YOU DON'T
HAVE TO
LEARN THE
HARD WAY

YOU DON'T HAVE TO LEARN THE HARD WAY

Making it in the *Real* World:
A Guide for Graduates

J. R. PARRISH

BENBELLA

BenBella Books, Inc.
Dallas, Texas

BENBELLA

BenBella Books, Inc.
6440 N. Central Expressway, Suite 503
Dallas, TX 75206
www.benbellabooks.com
Send feedback to feedback@benbellabooks.com

Printed in the United States of America
10 9 8 7 6 5 4 3 2 1

Library of Congress Cataloging-in-Publication Data is available for this title.

ISBN 978-1933771-74-8

Proofreading by Yara Abuata
Cover design by DesignForBooks.com
Text design and composition by DesignForBooks.com
Printed by Bang Printing

Distributed by Perseus Distribution
perseusdistribution.com

To place orders through Perseus Distribution:
Tel: 800-343-4499
Fax: 800-351-5073
E-mail: orderentry@perseusbooks.com

Significant discounts for bulk sales are available.
Please contact Robyn White at robyn@benbellabooks.com or (214) 750-3600.

CONTENTS

PREFACE

This book was written specifically for recent high school and college graduates to provide them with a head start in life by teaching them how to function at an exceedingly high level in the real world with proven, time-tested principles. If you're willing to apply what you read in these pages, within a year, you'll be able to function at the level of someone ten years your senior. I realize that's a big assertion; however, I can say it with authority because of personal experience.

When I was in my twenties, I was privileged to have a mentor who told me he would grow me twenty years in one year—and he did.

My life has never been the same. So, if you're serious about making the most of your future, you're about to learn how. My objective is to give you the means to turn your goals and dreams into reality. I want you to become the person who hits the proverbial home run to win the game or sets an Olympic record. I will show you how to have your own Mercedes, live in a dream home near the sea with your own pool and tennis court, marry the person you love, and have your marriage be lasting and blissful. I'll provide you with tools that will allow you to live anywhere in the world, obtain a job that excites you each morning and leaves you fulfilled every evening, have ample money to live in financial peace, and be able to help others less fortunate than yourself.

As you read the following pages, you'll encounter the words *success* and *riches* frequently. It's important that you realize that money is only one measurement of success and riches. You're rich and successful when you have good health, a loving family, close friends, a pleasing personality, a job you love doing, and the ability to help others. Keep those definitions in mind as you measure your progress. You can achieve your dream life with a reasonable amount of effort. It will take self-discipline, but a life without self-discipline can't be a good life. You will learn to function in ways that will benefit you in all areas of your life. It's important to learn that much of the joy you'll receive in life will come from being a blessing to others. You will profit directly from what you learn; however, you will also be shown how to bless others, a skill that's vital to having the wonderful future you desire and deserve.

To the best of my knowledge, this is the first time a life guide this complete has been available in one book. If you're willing to put the things you'll be taught here into practice, you'll achieve more than you've ever thought possible. You'll learn how to deal effectively with people. You'll see how to acquire the habits that will make your dreams come true, how to find your ideal mate and be happy with him or her, how to satisfy your financial needs and make money work for you, and how to select the right career. You'll learn the importance of your thoughts and how to use that knowledge to enrich your life and the lives of others. You'll discover the importance of mentors—how to choose them as well as how to keep them and why. This book will also help you gain an understanding of the meaning of love and how to apply that knowledge to benefit your life and the lives of others. While you're still in your twenties, you'll have the advantage of knowing things I didn't learn until my forties.

Now, let's begin your journey to a beautiful future.

CHAPTER

HUMAN RELATIONS

At the beginning of each chapter, I'll share a personal story that illustrates the advice and information in the pages that follow.

It was a beautiful, sunny June day and I'd just stepped off the stage with my high school diploma in hand. My car was already packed. I never returned home again except to visit. I headed north from Escondido, California, to Los Angeles, where I was to have a tryout with a new major league baseball team, the Los Angeles Angels. It was an exhilarating day. I'd played baseball since I was five and I was good at it, so I had hopes of a major league career. When I arrived at the field, I took my first big gulp when they told all the infielders to take turns at shortstop. I was a second baseman and the throw from shortstop to first base was much longer than I was accustomed to. I was an excellent fielder but didn't have the arm of a shortstop. I was stunned at the number of players who could throw the baseball from that distance as if it were shot from a rifle. That was strike one. I was an outstanding hitter and did well in batting practice, which encouraged me. For the next drill, they had their stopwatches out, timing us as we ran the bases. Speed on the bases was a weakness of mine. Some of the others could run the bases like greyhounds, so that was strike two. To conclude the day, they separated us by age and experience. I was the only guy who just graduated from high school the day before. Strike three—and I was out.

I got into my car and headed north again, this time to Fresno, California. I'd been recruited to play baseball at Fresno State College. I played summer ball; to make money, I took a job soliciting customers for a local dairy's home delivery routes. They paid me five dollars for each new customer I signed up. In the fall, school started and I was growing optimistic about my future when a sad event occurred. Early one morning, one of the milk delivery drivers failed to see an approaching train in the darkness. It demolished his milk truck and killed him. The owner of the dairy needed someone to take over the man's business; I was the most logical candidate because I had recruited many of his customers, so I left college and went into the dairy business.

By now, you may be wondering what this story has to do with human relations. Hang in for a few more minutes and you'll understand the connection.

I was successful at the local dairy and was soon recruited by the largest dairy in Fresno to work in their home delivery unit. I signed up numerous new customers and they soon put me in charge of their twenty-six home delivery routes. Shortly after that, opportunity came knocking again. The owner of the dairy found it difficult to get his department heads to work together and couldn't entice his eldest son to work at the dairy. It was very important to him that both these events take place. He learned of a consultant in Seattle who had a superb record in building teams and managing people. He interviewed this man and hired him to solve his two problems.

The next thing I knew, I was being introduced to Glenn H. Lay and told he would be working with all the department heads to teach us teamwork. Glenn was a little overweight, balding, very friendly, about forty-five years old, and always had a big smile. He seemed to be a person who could teach me things

I needed to know. Little did I know the enormous influence he would have on the balance of my life.

Most of the department heads were much older than I was and were set in their ways. Most of them were not looking for help from Glenn or anyone else. This turned out to be a blessing for me.

You never know when your opportunities will come or what form they will take. A fundamental secret of success is to be ready for your opportunities when they appear. Opportunity does you no good if you're not in a position to take advantage of it. This important truth applies to all aspects of your life.

I'll never forget my first meeting with Glenn. He set the time for our meeting and arrived at my modest office a few minutes early. I felt like a big shot because this important man wanted to meet with me. He told me we were going to have our conversation in the owner's office. I'd never been invited to the owner's office and was delighted. We walked through the administration area and down a long hall, arriving at a massive door. Glenn opened the door and stepped to one side, motioning me to enter. I didn't understand that by this act he was demonstrating one of the fundamentals of good human relations: *Let others go first.*

I held my shoulders back and marched through the door as if I owned the place. I was about to sit down in one of the plush chairs in front of the owner's desk when Glenn motioned to me to sit behind the desk in the owner's chair. I thought I was having an out-of-body experience but jumped at the opportunity. By this time, I was feeling puffed up and powerful and sitting in the owner's chair added more fuel to the fire. I settled into the most comfortable chair I'd ever sat in while Glenn perched in one of the chairs in front of the desk. He sat in a way that allowed him to look up at me, causing me to look down at him. That was also significant in terms of human relations skills, but of course I had no idea about any of that at the time. All I would have needed then was a glass of brandy, a cigar, and a private jet to feel I had become one of the rich and famous. We talked for an hour or rather, I should say, he asked questions and I talked. Finally, he ended the questions and told me there was a word I needed to learn if I was going to be a success. I was pleased and interested, but he wouldn't reveal the word. He gave me clues and worked with me for a few minutes, but I still had no idea what word he was expecting. Finally, I pleaded with him just to tell me. He stalled a bit longer, then told me the word was *humility.* I promptly asked him what it meant. I had no clue about the meaning of the word and no humility to boot.

A few weeks passed and Glenn appeared at my office again, saying he had something important to discuss. He told me he had signed a one-year contract and that most of the department heads were stubborn and hard to work with. He said he wanted to focus a lot of his attention on me because I was eager to learn. Then he dropped the bomb. He said if I would do exactly as he asked for the next twelve months, he would grow me *twenty years* in *one year*.

After recovering from my initial surprise, I immediately told him he had a deal. His plan was to teach me human relations, but I didn't even know what the words meant. Glenn had a master's degree in human relations and was at least twenty years ahead of his time back in the sixties. At the end of our year, Glenn had induced the owner's son to work at the dairy and done a remarkable job teaching the department heads to perform as a team. He also grew me the twenty years he had promised. He left the dairy and so did I. My life rocketed up the ladder of success from that point forward.

This brings us to why those of you who want success and happiness need to understand human relations.

It must be a win–win situation to be effective. When I met Glenn, I generally thought people were a pain and preferred to be on my own. I didn't realize my future success would depend on how effective I was in dealing with people and that I needed the help of others to achieve that success. I learned that technical skills were important, but the best jobs and promotions went to the people with the greatest human relations skills. Once I fully grasped this concept and began applying these skills, my life improved in a hurry. I felt like I'd discovered the Comstock Lode (one of the largest silver discoveries in the history of America). I had been taught a primary principle for success. I kept in touch with Glenn. One day I told him how well things were going and how amazed I was by the way people had changed. He informed me that it was not they who had changed—it was me.

Practicing good human relations means giving another person what he or she wants in order to get what you want. It means keeping the other person's ego intact at all times. Learning human relations skills is the fastest way to improve every aspect of your life.

At this point, I should tell you that Glenn's life did not turn out the way I would have expected. He got off course later in his life and failed to apply many of the principles he had taught me. He got divorced, got in trouble with the IRS, and caused himself many other serious difficulties. None of this detracts from the importance of the principles he taught. Even though his life went in a direction I would never have expected, his wisdom had its own legacy, which was my success and the fact that I've carried on the work he started. It shows the impact one person can have on another's life.

Glenn's later difficulties illustrate another important truth: life is not always neat and clean. Mentors are human and subject to the same temptations as others, but their wisdom is priceless. Don't expect that your mentor will be perfect—none of us are. As these pages will show, I have made many mistakes. Learn the lessons mentors can teach you, always remembering that they are also human.

You have a huge advantage because you're young and will have the opportunity to apply the skills you're about to learn for the rest of your life. The principles you'll acquire in this chapter will make you a standout in every aspect of life. If these skills could propel me from an ordinary job as a milkman to being the top salesman in the United States for a Fortune 500 company,

Your future will be determined by how effectively you learn to deal with people.

allow me to start my own real estate company, and retire in Hawaii at age fifty-five, imagine what they can do for you. For further proof of the importance of human relations skills, all you have to do is look at today's reality television shows and ask yourself why one individual gets selected for the job over all of the competition or why someone wins a million dollars by becoming the sole survivor. In each case, you'll see it was because the winner dealt more effectively with people than the other contestants did. Now, let's start sharing the information that will take you to the top, allowing you to be a frontrunner in life.

MENTORS

As you reflect on the story you just read about how I grew twenty years in one year, it will be apparent that the right mentor can open the door to your success. Before getting into our discussion on human relations, I'm going to suggest a few basics for finding and keeping your own mentor.

1. A mentor is a channel to wisdom and the goodwill of others. A good mentor acts like a filter to help you avoid costly mistakes and guide you through the perilous waters of life.
2. It's important to select a mentor you like and respect.
3. Keep in mind that your mentor will appreciate the fact that you trust, respect, and admire him or her. Believing in a mentor is a compliment.

④ Don't confuse a mentor with a role model.
Mentors are people who work with you one
on one and have your best interests at heart.
They develop a vested interest in your success
and care about you as a person. Role models
usually play no intimate role in your life, such as
sports figures or entrepreneurs who you admire
and respect. You don't know these people and
sometimes they disappoint. Role models are
common and unpredictable. Finding the right
mentor is like discovering a rare diamond.

⑤ You may want more than a single mentor. Perhaps you'll choose one for finance or real estate
and another who has a track record in personal
relationships such as friendship and marriage.

⑥ Once you find your mentor, it's essential that you
show respect and never become a "Yeah, but." If
your mentor tells you your hair is too long and
needs to be cut, do it. Don't ever say, "Yeah, but I
had it short and that didn't help." Whatever your
mentor suggests, do it and do it immediately if
you want him or her to continue to help you. It's
one thing to do what your mentor suggests and
report back how it went and quite another to
question the advice without trying it. You won't
last long if you resist suggestions.

7 If you want to keep your mentor, make sure you thank him or her and show appreciation for the smallest things your mentor does for you. Report the results each time you follow your mentor's advice.

8 Bring small gifts and send personal, hand-written, thank-you notes for the advice and counsel you receive from your mentor.

We will discuss mentors further as we go along.

OTHERS

You're living in the most complex era in the history of the world. Simplicity has nearly vanished at the expense of multitasking and endless choices. The ability to keep things simple is the path to inner peace and satisfaction. For that reason, I was determined to reduce the secret to success in life down to one word. After many hours of thought, it came to me: *others*. When you begin focusing on others, good things start happening to you. An essential paradigm for success is realizing and accepting how indispensable people are to your future.

No enduring achievement is possible without the help of other people. Interdependency is as necessary for success and happiness as water is to life. You'll eventually understand that everything you do for others, you're also doing for your-

Your success or failure will be determined first and foremost by how effectively you deal with others.

self. The fact that you benefit from these acts is not the driving motivation for helping others because helping them is its own reward; however, the fact that you do benefit is a bonus. Have you ever considered the fact that without other people, no one is going to pick up your trash, clean your teeth, cure your illnesses, provide your groceries, supply your electricity, build your computer, your house, and your car, and provide all your security and emergency services?

The way you are treated by other people will depend on your human relations skills. If people admire and respect you, feel good when they're with you, they'll help you to have a better

Every facet of life requires the support of other people.

life. They will promote you, give you raises, and look out for you in unusual ways. The person you want to date or marry will be attracted to you. The people you want as friends will become your friends. It's unusual for young people to comprehend the importance of others fully, so you will have a great advantage when you become one of the few who does.

By helping others, you build a network of people who will help you in turn. That network evolves as the people you help extol your

The fastest way to achieve your own goals is to help others achieve theirs.

virtues to their friends and families, thereby building your reputation. As your standing grows, you'll be amazed how many people seek you out. *Others* are the unconditional element you need to have a bright future. I found that concept so important that I still have that word on my car's license plate and on a

You may be surprised to learn that you already possess what other people desperately want.

plaque in my office as a constant reminder to think of others. Now that you are aware of the significance of other people, your mission is to learn how to deal with them successfully.

The best news of all is that as you give people what they want, you don't lose any of what you gave away. The balance of this chapter is devoted to teaching you how to give others what they yearn for while getting what you want from them at the same time.

EVERYONE'S GREATEST NEED

If you knew the greatest need of every person on earth other than food, clothing, and shelter, you would likely

Everyone's greatest need after food, clothing, and shelter is **The Need to Feel Important.**

be able to figure out how to deal effectively with anyone. Imagine how successful you could be if you knew how to satisfy the greatest need of every person with whom you come in contact. It may amaze you to learn that you can.

If you put this one concept into practice, you will immediately begin to improve your life.

1. You will win or lose with people in direct proportion to your ability to satisfy their need to feel important.
2. This concept is your key to dealing effectively with people.
3. Nothing you can do will be more important to your future than learning good human relations.
4. This revelation was the first major turning point of my life.

You must become comfortable with who you are before you can focus on others.

Now let's concentrate on learning ways to make people feel important. You already have that ability. Most people don't realize what makes others feel important because they're too busy trying to make themselves feel important. Usually this is not a conscious act.

If your ego is hungry for attention and power, and most people's are, it's almost impossible to focus on others. That's one of the reasons so few people practice good human relations. When I learned I already had what others wanted and all I had to do was give it to them and they would like and want to help me, it was pretty easy to take my attention off myself.

To make sure I thought of others, I imagined the initials **MMFI** *on everyone's forehead. Those initials stand for* **Make Me Feel Important.**

It became easy to focus on others because it was effective; the more I made them feel important, the more I succeeded. I felt better about myself each time I made the other person feel good and I realized I had an unlimited reserve to keep on giving. With repetition, satisfying the needs of others to feel important soon became a habit. I've been applying this principle for more than forty years and it's just as effective today as it was in the 1960s.

You now know the secret of how to succeed with people, so let's see how to apply it.

THE SPOTLIGHT

From the time we're small children, we start looking for the spotlight. One of the first things children crave is to have Daddy and Mommy watch them perform. A spotlight on anyone signals importance. Children want to feel like the actor taking center stage or the man and woman on the high trapeze. Being in the limelight makes us feel important. The problems arise when people mature and continue wanting to keep the spotlight on themselves. To practice good human relations, you must put the spotlight on the person you want to impress. You'll be amazed at their reaction and desire to spend more time with you. Here are some proven ways to use that spotlight:

1. Talk about what they want to talk about.
2. Ask questions about them.
3. Show genuine interest in them.
4. Pay them sincere compliments.
5. Praise them for things you admire about them.
6. Put them first. Let them go through doors first, talk first, be first in line, and go first in every way.
7. Nod your agreement or say "me too" when they say things with which you agree.
8. Inquire about their hobbies, favorite foods, music, and movies.
9. See those initials—*MMFI*—on everybody's forehead and make them feel important.

Stop here and reflect on the people you like being around.

1. Do they focus on you?
2. Do they talk about your interests?
3. Do they ask lots of questions about you?
4. Do they do thoughtful things for you?
5. Do you like yourself better when you're around them?

You'll find them to be the ones who make you feel important. One of the greatest compliments anyone can pay you is to say *I like me best when I'm with you.*

That's how people will respond to you when you make them feel important. Begin putting the spotlight on others and watch your life improve.

YOUR SIX BEST FRIENDS

I can hear you saying to yourself: *what does this guy know about my six best friends?* I know a great deal about them and you may not know them very well yet. These are the friends you'll be calling upon to bail you out of uncomfortable circumstances and to assist you in making others feel important. You'll want these friends to play a major role in all of your future conversations. The names of your six best friends are *Who*, *What*, *Why*, *Where*, *When*, and *How*.

These are the friends that will help you learn about others and make them feel important. Whenever you want to remove the spotlight from yourself, you simply call on one of your friends. You'll use them like this: "Daniel, please tell me *how* you find the time to be so thoughtful? Shari, *where* did you learn such wonderful manners?" Each friend helps create conversation and keeps the spotlight on the other person. Each friend makes it difficult for the other person to answer *yes* or *no*. If you're attempting to keep a conversation going, you want to ask questions that can't be answered with just a *yes* or *no*. These are known as open-ended questions. One of the best ways to use them is to ask people how they feel. Feelings questions require a more detailed answer and open the door to more questions. With questions such as "Tammy, *how* do you feel about capital punishment?" Tammy can't answer simply *yes* or *no* and must elaborate. Learn to employ your six friends. I can't begin to count the times they've helped me. I use them daily and they never let me down. Embrace them and watch your popularity grow.

SMILE

Most boys are instructed to "act like a man," which rarely includes smile training. Girls seem to be taught the importance of smiling early in life and it pays big dividends for them. How often have you heard someone say that Lisa or Mika has a smile that can light up a room? A sincere smile conveys many subtle messages:

1 I'll be nice.
2 I'm friendly.
3 I like you.
4 You're worth pleasing.

Almost everyone responds warmly to a sincere smile. A smile happens quickly, but its effects can be lasting. A genuine smile helps create happiness in the home. It enriches each person who receives it while costing the giver nothing. Smiling makes everyone feel more relaxed and gives the one smiling an advantage by charming whoever he or she encounters. A smile isn't masculine or feminine—smiles work regardless of age. This is a trait you'll want to adopt immediately.

Smiling is one way to start winning with people without saying a word.

FIRST IMPRESSIONS

"You never get a second chance to make a good first impression." This famous saying, often attributed to humorist Will Rogers, points out the enduring quality of first impressions. If you're impressed with people the first time you meet them, you tend to keep liking them and will tolerate a lot before changing your opinion. The same is true about

A smile is an inexpensive way to improve your looks.

people you immediately dislike. It's very difficult for them to get into your good graces once they make a bad first impression. For those reasons, it's exceedingly important to know how to impress people the first time you meet them. Consider the number of people you'll need to impress because of the influence they'll have on your future. They include your teachers, coaches, the people who interview you for jobs, the people you want to date, and potential mentors.

So how do you make a good first impression? Not one person in a hundred can answer that question correctly. Most people think they impress others by the way they dress or by showing how smart they are. They also think name-dropping or talking about their accomplishments works. None of those actions will create a good first impression. There's only one sure way to make a good first impression: *show other people that you're impressed with them.*

Let's look at some of the best ways to accomplish that:

1   You begin by maintaining good eye contact—whether you're asking a question or listening. If that's difficult for you, and it is for most people at first, look right between their eyes. It feels to them as though you're looking in their eyes and reduces the intensity of direct eye contact until you become accustomed to it.

2   Show them your approval any time you can do so sincerely.

3   Be quick to say "me too" whenever they say things that are similar to the way you feel or act. For example, if they say they love to go to the ocean and you do also, you give them a "me too." The more they see that you are like them, the more impressed with you they will be.

4   Ask them questions (*remember your six friends*) about their lives and interests.

5 Ask them to expand on things they say that impress you.

6 Smile at them often and nod your agreement at every opportunity.

7 Be sure to stay agreeable and avoid criticism or interruption.

8 Finally, here's an important human relations rule: *talk about yourself only when invited to do so.*

I imagine that you're beginning to recognize that the practice of good human relations requires that you continually make others feel good about themselves.

LISTENING

Thoughtful listening is one of the most effective ways to make people feel important. Many arguments and misunderstandings between spouses, parents, children, and friends arise from one of them feeling like the other doesn't listen. Most people seem to prefer to do the talking; when they're not talking, they're frequently "reloading" instead of listening. Effective listening is a virtue that results in benefits that will improve your life. When I was working for Xerox, they sent me to their sales school in Rochester, New York. One of the skills they trained us in was effective listening. This ability has had immense value throughout my life. Few things make us feel less important than not being listened to. We feel resentful and disrespected when we're interrupted or made to feel that what we say isn't important. I'm sure you've found yourself in situations where you've been making what you thought was interesting conversation, only to be interrupted or ignored by someone looking away as you spoke, implying boredom with his or her body language. How did that make you feel? Probably not very important and I'm sure that person lost your respect. Those moves are human relations suicide. One of the new habits you'll want to acquire is being a good listener. Here's the best reason to become a good listener: *you can't learn anything while you're talking!*

So, if you lose with other people when you don't listen and you aren't learning anything when you're talking, doesn't it make sense to listen and win? Let's look at the traits effective listeners exhibit:

1. Look directly in the eyes of those doing the talking. Eye contact indicates to them that you're listening.
2. Stay with their subject as long as they are willing. You want them to know you don't want to miss a word they have to say.
3. Lean a little toward them as they speak.

④ Occasionally ask for clarification on things they say.

⑤ Ask them to tell you more about things that interest you.

⑥ Repeat some of the things they say back to them to be sure you understand.

⑦ Encourage them to keep talking.

⑧ Ask open-ended questions—questions that cannot be answered with a simple *yes* or *no*.

⑨ Nod your head with approval when you agree.

⑩ Ask if you can make some notes on things they say that seem significant.

⑪ Don't jump in when they pause for breath. Taking a long pause after they stop talking shows you're considering what they said.

Improve your human relations skills by becoming an effective listener.

QUIZ	HOW GOOD ARE YOU AT MAKING OTHERS FEEL IMPORTANT?

① When you go to your friend's house and his mother answers the door, you . . .

  a Say "Hi, is Alex home?" and head straight for your friend's bedroom.

b Say "Hi, Mrs. Jones, how are you doing today?" and listen to the answer even though you feel a little uncomfortable talking to older people for long.

c Make eye contact, ask how Mrs. Jones is doing, and stay for a few minutes to chat about what you're up to as well.

2 When you see that your friend is wearing new clothes, you . . .

a Say nothing about the clothes unless she mentions it.

b Ask if the clothes are new and say you like them.

c Tell your friend you like the clothes and she really looks good in them, even if you may not think they're the greatest.

3 When you're talking on the phone with a friend who is telling you about something bad that happened to him, you . . .

a Try to help him by pointing out what he should have done because you care and want him to do better next time.

b Tell him you know just how he feels and then talk about something similar that happened to you to distract him.

c Ask him some more questions about the situation, and let him know you're on his side no matter what.

QUIZ	**HOW GOOD ARE YOU AT MAKING OTHERS FEEL IMPORTANT?**

(continued)

4 After your team beats a friend's team, you . . .

a Joke around with her, telling her that her team really sucked.

b Talk really enthusiastically about how great your team did so she'll know her team didn't lose because they were bad, it was just that your team had better luck today.

c Accept congratulations and tell her that her team did a great job, too.

5 If you and your friends come across someone you know working in a fast food place, you . . .

a Kind of feel uncomfortable and pretend like you don't know him.

b Joke around with your friends about working in such a lame job.

c Stick up for him and tell your friends to stop putting him down.

6 If your friend tells you about how well she did on a big test, you . . .

a Say great, and then mention how you did great, too, without even studying.

b Tell her, "That's great," and change the subject to hide the fact that you feel a little competitive.

c Congratulate her and suggest you go out to celebrate the good news.

7 If your friend has a music or dance recital or some kind of performance, and you know he really wants you to come, you . . .

a Make up a really believable excuse not to go, so his feelings won't be hurt.

b Say you'll go to please your friend, but you can't help but act bored.

c Go and make an effort to be interested even though you're bored.

8 You know your friend is upset about something, but you don't know what it is, so you . . .

a Wait for her to bring up what's on her mind, so she won't think you're getting too personal.

b Ask what's up because she seems a little down but if she says nothing is wrong, leave it alone.

c Ask her if anything's bothering her and, even if she brushes you off at first, keep asking questions so she knows you really want to listen and help.

9 Your friends are all going to a New Year's Eve party and you don't have a date. Your friends find you a "date," but you're not really attracted to him/her, so you . . .

a Hang out as much you can with your friends to avoid both of you being uncomfortable.

| QUIZ | **HOW GOOD ARE YOU AT MAKING OTHERS FEEL IMPORTANT?** *(continued)* |

b Talk to your "date," but don't go out of your way because you don't want the person to think you're into him/her.

c Ask questions about what kind of music or movies he/she likes, and try to make the best of it.

10 Your cousin, the geek, is visiting your family and your parents want you to bring him to hang out with your friends. You . . .

a Tell your parents you wish you could but there is no way. You promise to be back in a few hours to hang out with him.

b Let him come but you're more worried about what your friends think than how your cousin feels.

c Introduce your cousin to your friends, after telling them privately that he's a geek but they should act nicely because he's your cousin.

| SCORE | Count up the number of times you answered a, b, and c, then flip to the end of the chapter to find out what your score means. |

STAGE SETTING

All the areas of human relations that we're covering are important, but this one rates particularly high because it's the best way to get what you want from others. Stage setting involves thinking through what you want to happen before meeting with someone and then creating an atmosphere that will compel the other person to go down the road you've chosen. It's designed as much to prevent what you don't want to happen as it is to get what you want. You set the stage by the first thing you say or do in a meeting. The best way to explain this is through an example.

Let's say you're a girl who wants a boy you like to take you to the prom. You know from experience that he resists going to dances. To set the stage properly, you'd begin the conversation like this: "Henry, the reason I asked you to give me ten minutes of your time with no interruptions is because I have something that is very important to me to discuss with you. One of the things I admire about you is you've always been willing to listen when I really needed your attention. You know if the tables were turned and you had a request of me, I'd consider thoughtfully anything that was important to you. This is one of the times when I'm trusting I can rely on you to have an open mind about something important to me." From there, you'd state your case—I can't imagine the person who would not give your request a try. Girls who don't understand stage setting would be defensive and inadvertently set a very different stage, something like: "Henry, I've asked you to take me to dances many times before and you always say no, but would you consider taking me to the prom?" This would almost guarantee another no. An interesting thing about stage setting is you're doing it whether you know it or not every time you meet with someone. Given that you're setting the stage no matter what you do, you'll be much better off knowing how to set it to get what you want. It becomes easy and natural with practice.

Proper stage setting involves thinking through what you want and don't want to happen and then setting up the conversation accordingly. If you're babysitting and it's time for the little girl to go to bed, and you know from experience that she usually resists, you could begin like this: "Nikki, I want you to know that I'm really proud of you. You've done all the things I've asked you to do tonight and with such a good attitude. I have a college report that's due tomorrow and I need your cooperation. I know you want me to get a good grade on my report and that you will be a good girl now and go brush your teeth and hop in bed. I'll be up in a few minutes to tuck you in."

Stage setting's an art, and when done properly, it will help you get what you want from others while leaving them feeling good. Remember to ask *yes* questions if you want *yes* answers and nod your head *yes* when you want a *yes* response. *Yes* questions are those that you know the other person will answer *yes* to, which puts him or her in a *yes* mood. Here are some examples of *yes* questions: you want your brother to have the best education possible, don't you? You want to ensure that your car doesn't break down again, don't you? Practice stage setting and you'll be the one with the big smile on your face as you find you're repetitively fulfilling your desires.

Just as with stage setting, we frequently don't get what we desire from a parent or friend because of the way we ask. For example, if you want your boyfriend to take you to the beach, there are a variety of ways you can ask, but the worst would be: "Kenny, I don't suppose you'd take me to the beach today, would you?"

Don't Ask *If*—ask *Which*.

That approach usually compels him to say *no*. Here's a better approach: "I've been thinking about you today and was wondering if you would go to the beach with me?" By that approach, you've made him feel modestly important by letting him know you were thinking about him and asked a *yes* question. To give yourself the best odds of getting the response you want, *don't ask if, ask* which.

Your best approach would go something like this: "Kenny, I've been thinking about us a great deal today, remembering the amazing times when we do things together. I know you prefer me to think things through before coming to you with my requests, so I've followed your advice and thought this through carefully. I've taken into consideration the things you like and what we might enjoy together. (This is where the *which* comes in and where you offer two choices, being confident which one he will choose.) I've identified two trips and want you to select *which* one you prefer. Would you rather take the beautiful scenic drive up to the lake and visit my mom and sister because we haven't seen them in such a long time or would you prefer just the two of us spend a romantic day at the beach on Saturday?" Let's assess what you've accomplished by this line of questioning:

Don't ask a no question if you want a yes answer.

1 You let him know you were thinking of past good times the two of you enjoyed.

2 You told him you took his advice and thought the request through before coming to him.

3 By asking *which,* you eliminated *no* as a possible answer.

4 You're letting him make the choice.

5 By asking about the visit, you gave him a choice you felt confident he wouldn't take, which left him choosing the alternative you wanted.

6 He will feel relieved at not having to go to your mom's and you'll feel happy going to the beach.

Another example of this method comes from my youth, when we would go to a soda fountain for a malted milk. The soda clerk's job was to sell eggs with the malted milk. If he didn't have the skills, he would shyly say, "You probably don't want an egg in your malted milk, do you?" The answer would be a quick *no.* If he knew what you now know, he would hold an egg in each hand and say, "*Which* do you prefer, one egg or two in your malted milk?" Normally, the answer would be the one he was looking for: "Oh, only one, please." Learn to get what you want from others by asking the questions with choices.

ARGUMENTS/TEMPERS

No matter how much human relations training you've had, you'll still occasionally find yourself in an uncomfortable situation with someone who wants to argue or who has lost his or her temper. Once you've learned good human relations skills, you'll know how to handle the situation.

Let's take a look at the process:

1. Speak quietly and softly. The level of your voice will dictate how the other person responds. If you're shouted at, you'll usually shout back. If you lower your voice, the other person will lower his or hers. In a tense situation, it's normal for voices to rise and tempers to flare. Take the lead from the beginning and speak quieter and softer than normal.

2. Hear the other person out. When arguments begin, it's natural to want to get your point across. The most prudent move to defuse the situation is keeping the person who is

upset talking as long as you can. Keep asking questions (never forget your six friends) that demonstrate you want to understand his or her point of view.

3 When the other person is done, ask if there's anything else he or she can add.

4 Pause a moment before stating your case. You want the other person to know that you carefully considered what was said and aren't just trying to prove him or her wrong.

5 When you state your case, do it in a quiet voice and keep it as succinct and simple as possible.

6 Be content if you both move toward common ground. Even if you only agree on 50 percent of the contested points, it's progress and should be appreciated. Never insist on winning 100 percent.

7 Let the person know that you would likely have felt the same way had you been in his or her shoes. That attitude will go a long way toward keeping the other person's ego intact.

It's best to avoid arguments entirely, but at least now you know what to do next time you're put on the spot.

QUIZ	DO YOU FIGHT FAIR?

1 When you get really mad at a friend, you call them names to their face.

☐ Yes   ☐ No

2 When an argument gets heated, you walk away because you're afraid you'll say something terrible.

☐ Yes   ☐ No

3 When someone gives you a hard time, you often raise your voice and feel like hitting them.

☐ Yes   ☐ No

4 When you're fighting with someone about one thing, and they start throwing other stuff in your face that has nothing to do with it, you do the same thing.

☐ Yes   ☐ No

5 After an argument's over, you feel worse than before.

☐ Yes   ☐ No

SCORE	Give yourself 1 point for every YES and 5 points for every NO, then flip to the end of the chapter to find out what your score means.

PRAISE

After forty years of studying and applying human relations, I've come to realize that one of the most effective ways to get along with others is through the use of praise. Praise is comparable to a miracle drug and it's applied very sparingly in our society. Just ask yourself how much praise you've received in the past week. People whose egos aren't strong have a hard time giving praise. They appear to feel that if they praise someone, it makes them look weak. Nothing could be further from the truth.

Praise greatly enhances the well-being and confidence of the person receiving it. For winning with others, there are few acts that can match praise. Few things make us feel better than for someone to tell us how good we look, what a fine job we did, or why they like being with us. One benefit of bestowing praise is that it makes the other person want to continue the desired behavior so he or she can get more approval. This brings us to an exceptionally important concept: *whenever you observe a desired behavior from your boyfriend or girlfriend, parent, sibling, friend, or anyone you want to win with, always reinforce that behavior with praise.*

When you praise people, it makes them feel good; it makes you look good and feel fantastic.

For example, let's say your girlfriend moves over and sits close to you while you are driving with her and occasionally gives you a hug and kiss on the cheek. If you want her to continue this behavior, nothing will accomplish it more surely than praise. Say something like: "Shirley, I can't tell you how wonderful it made me feel when you moved over close to me while we were driving yesterday. Not only was it thoughtful, it was very romantic. If there's anything you'd like me to do for you, it would make my day. I'm lucky to have such a thoughtful girlfriend. I love you very much."

Giving sincere praise causes other people to want to be around you. Praise makes us feel as good as criticism makes us feel bad. No one wants to be with someone who's always criticizing. Almost everyone wants to be around the person who's looking for the good and praising it. Most people have grown up looking for what's wrong instead of what's right. Form the habit now of looking for the good in everything and everyone. When you do, you'll feel great about yourself and others will be attracted to you. You'll be surprised at all the places you find good once you're looking for it. You'll start noticing an attractive dress, a smart observation, a thoughtful deed, a kind word, a loving act, and much more. Life is full of good and favorable things once you're looking for them. Practice praise and you'll become like the pied piper with a line of people wanting to follow you.

CONTRADICTING/CRITICIZING

Benjamin Franklin said, "All my life I denied myself the pleasure of contradiction." As you may know, Benjamin Franklin was one of the most persuasive people in America's history. He was a great diplomat and master of human relations. He attributed much of his success to avoiding contradicting people unless someone's welfare was at stake. Arguing against others is a sure way to lose with them. I understand there are times when you have to contradict someone, but they are rare. Most contradicting is done to prove you know the correct answer and that the

Only contradict if there could be bad consequences if you don't.

other person is mistaken. For example, let's say someone states that we have only had four inches of rain this year. You know for a fact that we've had six inches. If you don't understand human relations, you may respond, "No, we've had six inches of rain this year, not four." How does that make the other person look and feel? *Generally speaking, if you're contradicting, you're losing.*

What difference does it make whether it was four or six inches of rain so far this year? Before you contradict again, ask yourself whether it matters. If the answer is no (and it usually is), hold your tongue. However, if you're at a swimming hole and someone's about to jump off a bluff and says the water is deep and there are no hidden rocks, but you know this is not true, by all means, contradict.

Criticism is contradiction's brother. It's best to criticize as infrequently as possible. A good rule is:

When you're tempted to criticize, bite your tongue.

Criticism is like a boomerang because it finds its way back to its sender. Rarely will you win with anyone if you're being critical. A critical spirit is frequently a mean spirit. Most often, criticism is not given to help the other fellow but in an attempt to boost the ego of the one doing the criticizing. A tendency to criticize is a common trait among neurotic, unhappy people. I repeatedly ask myself, "Who am I that I should judge another?"

A key thing to consider before delivering any criticism is your purpose in doing so. Are you really saying this to help the other person? Even if your answer is yes, the next thing to consider is whether the other person wants your help. Unless both answers are yes, it's best to steer clear of criticism entirely. If you decide to proceed, here are some guidelines that will help keep the other person's ego intact:

1. First and foremost, all criticism must be given in private. You trample on someone's ego when you criticize him or her in front of anyone else. It's human relations suicide. This applies to children as well as adults. If you must criticize your child, take him or her aside so others cannot hear what you're saying.

2. Preface any criticism with some of the things the person is doing right.

3. Be certain to criticize the act and not the person. If Aryel keeps leaving the refrigerator door open, you'll want to explain to her that leaving the door open causes problems with the food and the electric bill, but never say that she's stupid or dumb for doing it.

4. Be sure you only give one criticism per offense. It really hurts when someone starts in on one of our shortcomings and then pulls out a list of our past offenses.

5. Finally, you'll want to end any criticism with a positive thought and on a kind note. You may

do that by letting the person know that you've had to learn the same lesson.

As you grow in your human relations mastery, you'll put aside criticism, complaining, whining, condemning, and any form of judging others.

ALL I GIVE IS GIVEN TO MYSELF

Employing this concept will help you in many ways, not the least of which is getting along with others better. My desire is for you to comprehend the truth of this principle and apply it to the way you deal with others. The value is *whatever you are giving to others, you are also giving to yourself.*

If you give a smile or frown to someone, you usually get the same in return. If you give a welcoming attitude or a dismissive attitude, you get the same back. If you give distrust, you in turn are distrusted. If you give praise, you get praise. So the perplexing question is: *why do people go around giving what they don't want?* It must be because they don't understand that all they are giving is returned to them. Once you know you're going to get back what you give, the sensible person starts giving only what he or she wants to receive. Give love, peace, honesty, thankfulness, empathy, humility, grace, respect, trust, and kindness, and you'll be the recipient of the same gifts. Learn to give what you want to receive and start receiving the results you want. When you are getting what you don't want from others, make an assessment of what you've been giving to cause that result.

HELP OTHERS GET WHAT THEY WANT

One of the most effective ways ever discovered to get what you want is first to help others get what they want. By helping others get what they want, you build your public identity. In my real estate business in the 1970s, less than a year after starting the company, I met a man who was having difficulty selling a building he owned. He drove a fifteen-year-old Lincoln Continental, was about seventy-five years old, wore a suit and hat, and used a walking cane. Over the next few weeks, I learned all I could about him and his problem building. Because I had a genuine interest in solving his problem, he began to like me. I eventually sold his building and we became good friends. I was astonished when he told me one day that he was putting me on a monthly retainer to help him with his real estate needs. We began seeing each other for lunch every Wednesday and continued that tradition for five years until he passed on. In his last years, with his blessing, I was calling him Grandfather, because he had become the grandfather I had never had. He taught me more than anyone else I've ever met. When he passed away, he left me the same inheritance that he left his only son, a life estate, meaning I would receive a payment each month for the rest of my life. It's now been more than thirty years and I still get a monthly check. Those checks have already amounted to more than a million dollars and they will continue for the rest of my life. The things he taught me have been worth much more than the money and a great deal of what I'll be sharing with you came directly from him. That story shows how helping others get what they want can enhance your life.

APPRECIATION

One sure way to win with others is to show them appreciation. This is a virtue that seems so basic and yet it's not commonly applied. Have you thought about what it means to appreciate? When a house or other investment appreciates, what happens to it? It goes up in value. *When you show people appreciation, you raise them in value.*

The appreciative person will rarely lack friends. When you show appreciation, the receiver wants to do other nice things for you. Have you had the experience of buying a lunch or dinner, giving a gift, or doing some other thoughtful deed for someone and that person never gave you a simple thank you? It's a common occurrence these days and I don't know why. The more you show appreciation, the more the other party respects you, wants to be around you, and desires to help you. When you don't say thank you, people wonder why they did anything for you in the first place. I'm giving you this information based on a great deal of personal experience. I'm appalled at the lack of appreciation in our society today. It's as if many in our country have developed an entitlement mentality. Believe me, no one owes you anything and any kind deeds done for you deserve acknowledgment. Make sure that you show appreciation for any kind action done for you; it will increase your stature and reputation.

Becoming a person who accepts others as they are has a beneficial effect on people similar to appreciation. Be the person who accepts others as they are because you want to be accepted the way you are. You make people feel special and good about themselves when you accept them as they are. To go even further and really make others feel important, show your approval of them and their actions whenever you can. When you tell Paul how thoughtful and kind he was to bring donuts for the staff or to wait with an umbrella for you so you didn't get wet, you're winning with him by making him feel good about himself and about you. Each time you appreciate, accept, or approve of others, you are building their self-esteem as well as increasing the goodwill they have toward you. If you want to win with others, *be quick to show appreciation for their kind acts toward you.*

LIVE AND LET LIVE

I often thought that if I ever wrote another book, the title would be *Live and Let Live.* That tells you the significance I place on this concept. Learning to live and let live is one of the best gifts we can give ourselves and others. Much of the pain and suffering in this world is caused by one person telling others how to live their lives or what they should believe. You don't want anyone telling you what church to go to or when to cut your hair. How we live our lives is a personal choice and one of our basic rights. Yet there are people at every turn trying to tell you what you should and shouldn't do and what's right and wrong for you. They tell you what kind of car you should buy, how to raise your children, and how to treat your spouse. They tell you who to vote for, and what music to listen to, and the list goes on forever. I suggest that you make an honest assessment of how you conduct your life. Be frank with yourself and decide if you've learned the important lesson that others have the same right as you do to live their lives the way they see fit. If they are asking for your help or advice, by all means give it, but offering unsolicited advice is a horrible habit. Each of us has a full-time job just in improving ourselves. It reminds me of the lyrics of a country and western song: "If you mind your own business, you won't be minding mine." This virtue alone will make your company highly desired by others. Learn to live and let live.

BLAME

We can't leave our study of human relations without a discussion of blame. I'll call the first part of this discussion *The Better World Theory.*

If you're not happy with any-thing in your life, it's up to you and you alone to change it. You're **There's no one else to blame for your problems now or ever.** exactly where you are today because of your own choices.

Blaming anyone else is simply avoiding your responsibility. Make this your new motto:

If it's to be, it's up to me.

Once you accept this concept, you move from the passenger's seat to the driver's seat of your life. When you blame others, you're merely along for the ride. By accepting responsibility when you're unhappy about anything, you put yourself in a position to take action to make it better. If you don't accept responsibility, you'll likely whine and complain and feel the problem is someone else's fault. It's best to accept the fact that there is no one responsible for your problems but you. One way to determine if you're a blamer is to evaluate your level of anger.

For example, let's say you loan some money to friends to help them purchase a home. Your agreement is that they will pay you back in four months. When the time comes to pay you back, they tell you the money they were going to use to pay you back had to be spent on some repairs. You had planned on getting the money back to resolve one of your own debts and now you have a serious problem. You blame your friends and are angry with them. At this point, a wise person will realize that he or she wasn't forced to loan the money. You made that choice of your own free will. By loaning the

Most anger distills down to blame. When you eliminate blame, you eliminate anger.

money, you got yourself into the situation that's causing you pain. The only sensible approach is to accept
full responsibility for making the loan and all that
goes with it. By accepting responsibility, you'll have no
blame or anger and will simply deal with what needs
to be done, knowing it was created by your choices.

I recognize it isn't easy to adopt this advice. I
accepted full responsibility for my life when I was
twenty-three years old and it was one of the hardest
decisions I'd ever made. Maybe hearing how I eliminated blame from my life can help you follow suit.
You may recall I was working at a dairy in Fresno,
California, and was in charge of twenty-six home
delivery routes. I was punctual, fair, hard-working,
and generally an exemplary employee. No one needed
to look over my shoulder and I fulfilled my responsibilities with pride. I often served as a relief driver
covering routes for men on their days off. That gave
me the opportunity to learn all the routes and evaluate how the men were doing with their bookkeeping
and the maintenance of their trucks. We had a driver
who had worked at the dairy for twenty-six years. He
would occasionally get drunk and not show up for
work. I'd get a call at three o'clock in the morning and
have to go down to the dairy, load his truck, deliver
his milk, and make his collections. You can imagine

my mood after one of these episodes. I began having high anxiety and blaming this man for making my life miserable. One day when it had happened again, I was livid and raging when Glenn appeared at my office door. I began telling him how horrible my life had become because of Mr. Tequila. I recall Glenn looking me straight in the eye and saying something that troubled me: "I hate to tell you this, but you're blaming the wrong person." He went on to explain the better world theory to me and how the problem was with me and not with Mr. Tequila. I thought I must be hearing things. How on earth could it be my fault? Wasn't I the one getting out of bed on my day off and doing the job of this irresponsible man?

Glenn went on to tell me that life is always about choices and if you don't like the way something is, it's up to you to change it.

I asked him to clarify how this could possibly be *my* problem. He reminded me that I was the manager and that I had several courses of action: I could confront, warn, or fire my problem driver. He went on to say I could also keep running the route for him and stop complaining about it. He let me know I could resign from the dairy.

Even though I literally had a knot in my stomach, I began to see his point. A few days later, I called Mr.

Tequila into my office and had a long discussion with him about fulfilling his responsibilities. I informed him the next time he did not come into work without notice that he would be firing himself and that he need not even talk to me about it. I told him simply to come in and

He told me I could never again blame anyone else for my problems.

clean out his locker. He never again failed to do his job. I took intelligent action and it's now been more than forty years since I've blamed anyone for my problems. Eliminate blame and you'll have a much happier and more joyous life.

Before we leave the subject of human relations, here is a list of ways to make people feel important:

1. Be on time.
2. Send handwritten thank-you notes. An email message or text message does not carry the same weight.
3. In the presence of others, turn off your cell phone.
4. Use someone's name when addressing him or her.
5. Smile.
6. Return calls promptly.
7. Compliment.

8. Use good manners, such as standing when someone enters the room.

9. Dress appropriately.

10. Give honest answers.

11. Remember special days such as birthdays and anniversaries.

12. Respond quickly to requests.

13. Return anything borrowed promptly, especially money.

14. Be generous.

15. Be courteous.

16. Listen carefully.

17. Be respectful.

18. Be friendly.

19. Show compassion.

20. Be enthusiastic about ideas.

21. Laugh at jokes.

22. Offer a firm handshake.

23. Keep promises.

24. Let them know you're like them when appropriate.

25. Talk about their interests.

26. Express an interest in their background.

27. Show them you care about their future.

QUIZ   ARE YOU A BLAMER?

1 Your friend begs you to borrow $50 and you give in, even though you know he owes money to a lot of other people. You . . .

  a Get angry when your friend hasn't paid you back three months later.

  b Don't know whether to be madder at your friend or at yourself for letting him talk you into the loan.

  c Realize that you should be upset with yourself for making a bad choice and tell yourself not to let it happen again.

2 You get a speeding ticket while driving with your friends. You . . .

  a Get mad at your friends because even though you know you shouldn't speed, they kept saying hurry up.

  b Make excuses next time your friends ask you to drive them because you're afraid they'll get you into trouble again.

  c Decide that no matter who is in the car or what they say, you won't speed.

3 Your mom asks you to pick something up at a store and you get a parking ticket. You . . .

  a Hand the ticket to your mom, knowing she'll pay it because you got it doing her a favor.

b Tell your mom that you don't think it's fair that anybody should pay the ticket because the signs were really messed up.

c Show your mom the ticket, telling her you'll pay it—and hoping that she'll offer to help you out.

4 You fail a big test. You . . .

a Aren't going to beat yourself up about it because a lot of other kids failed it, too.

b Can't understand what happened because you studied really hard the night before.

c Get really upset with yourself.

5 You have a party at your house when your parents are out of town and the place gets trashed. You . . .

a Are furious at your friends.

b Tell your parents the truth—that you only invited a few friends over and somehow it got out of hand.

c Tell your parents you're sorry and ask what you can do to earn their trust again.

SCORE Count up the number of times you answered a, b, and c, then flip to the end of the chapter to find out what your score means.

CONCLUSION

If you asked me what improved my life most significantly and brought success, the answer would undoubtedly be learning effective human relations. We don't often use algebra, physics, history, or geography, but our success and happiness every single day of our lives depend on how well we get along with others. It's long been my dream to see human relations taught in every middle school, high school, and college in the United States. What could we possibly teach our youngsters that would be of greater value? What good does it do to fill our children's heads with knowledge if we don't teach them to have the confidence in themselves to implement it? I'm hopeful that once you put the principles you've learned into practice and experience the abundance and joy they bring you, you'll want to pass these important lessons on to those you love.

This is one of your moments of truth. You either start applying what you've learned so far or you are satisfied simply to have read the chapter.

If human relations training could propel me from being a milkman to the owner of my own company and on to early retirement in Hawaii, think what it can do for you.

Reading is one thing and acting on what you read is quite another. The reason my mentors said they helped me so much was that I acted on their advice. Only action will allow you to benefit from what you've learned from these pages. One of the unusual things about this chapter is that you can test its advice immediately by applying it to your own life. When put into practice, each of the principles you've read about will give you direct confirmation that you're on the right track. Now, let's see how much you've retained of what you read.

QUIZ   ANSWERS

● **HOW GOOD ARE YOU AT MAKING OTHERS FEEL IMPORTANT?**

What your score means:

MOSTLY As: You could use some serious practice in making others feel good. Once you figure out that you aren't the only person who needs to feel important, more people will want to hang out with you.

MOSTLY Bs: You're well on your way to making people like to be with you. Keep up the good work.

MOSTLY Cs: You're really good at making other people feel good about themselves. Keep on doing what you're doing because when you make others feel good, they'll want to help you out in return.

● DO YOU FIGHT FAIR?

What your score means:

If you scored 5 points or below, you need some practice on how to fight fair, so you can learn how to get past problems in relationships.

If you scored between 9 and 13 points, you're doing OK, but you could use some work on how to handle yourself when you encounter people who don't agree with you.

If you scored between 14 and 24 points, you are very good at resolving differences—you do well under pressure.

If you scored 25 points, you are great at handling disagreements—they could use you in the Middle East peace negotiations!

● ARE YOU A BLAMER?

What your score means:

MOSTLY As: You still need to figure out that when you take risks, there can be consequences you didn't expect, but you still have to deal with them.

MOSTLY Bs: You've figured out that you have to take responsibility for your own actions, even though sometimes it's easier to pass the buck.

MOSTLY Cs: You are doing a great job. You understand that you and only you are in charge of your life—and you feel pretty good about yourself for stepping up.

CHAPTER

2

HABITS

'm going to tell you a story that brings me great
shame, but I want you to hear it in the hope that my
foolishness may save you pain some day. It was Cinco
de Mayo and I left home around seven o'clock for my
Saturday morning golf game. It was a typical overcast
morning in Santa Cruz, California. We had only played
six holes when it began to rain. Soon, it was pouring
and there was no way to continue our round. All eight
of us sloshed back to the clubhouse at Pasatiempo Golf
Club and decided to start a dice game. It was cold, so
we got a blaze going in the fireplace and ordered drinks.
Someone suggested cognac and amaretto. I'd never had
this combination, but it did warm us up. We played
dice and drank right through the lunch hour.

It wasn't long before all of us were soused. It was now three in the afternoon, and after six hours of dice and drinking, I decided it was time to go home. My house was only two miles from the club. I staggered from the table out to my car and drove down the steep hill toward my house. I was driving a new Mercedes, but in my altered state, I neglected to put on my seatbelt. I made the right turn at the bottom of the hill and proceeded to drive head-on into a eucalyptus tree. The next thing I remembered was lying on the ground with red lights flashing all around me. There were two highway patrol cars, a fire truck, and an ambulance. It all looked quite strange from my vantage point, flat on my back. The paramedics slid me into the ambulance and rushed me to the hospital. The only thing I had on me was my money clip but no form of identification. I have no idea why I told them my name was Jack Parker and that I was twenty-six years old, but that's how I was registered at the hospital and that's who they thought they operated on. I had broken my hip, so when they operated, they had to insert two screws to hold it together. My head had smashed the windshield and I had bent both sides of the steering wheel all the way back to the steering column, which had not done my wrists much good.

Now it was seven in the evening and my wife was looking for me. She didn't find me until noon the following day because I was registered as Jack Parker and she was looking for J. R. Parrish. I'm telling you this story to introduce the importance of good habits. If I'd had the seatbelt habit, I would not have broken my hip and my head wouldn't have gone through the windshield. If I'd had the habit of moderation, I wouldn't have had the accident at all. I was terrified, ashamed, and humiliated by what I'd done and tormented for years by what could have happened. What if the tree had been a child or a family? I could have destroyed lives, spent years in prison, and probably never recovered psychologically. With just a little more speed, I would have been killed or paralyzed. Had I been on a freeway, there is no telling how much damage I might have done. Drinking and driving is a serious matter and a horrible habit. Make sure you don't fall into this trap because you almost certainly will not be as fortunate as I was.

You've no doubt considered habits as a part of everyone's life, but you may not have realized that your success or failure will depend on your habits. Og Mandino, the author of *The Greatest Salesman in the World*, which has sold more than two million copies, said, "Good habits are the key to all success and bad habits are the unlocked door to failure."

As an example, let's examine the habit of persistence. There are the minority who persist until they succeed and the many who quit at the first sign of resistance. If you don't persist, you can't succeed because *failure is a prerequisite to success.*

No matter what you're attempting to accomplish, you must stumble and fall before you learn how to succeed. Consider how often a baby falls while learning to walk. Losers quit at the first sign of difficulty. That old saying is true: "Quitters never win and winners never quit." The habit of persistence is essential to achievement. Each habit we discuss has its own significance and will aid in your march to success and happiness.

It's been proven that only a habit can subdue another habit. To relieve yourself of a bad habit, you must replace it with a good one. Forming any habit requires repetition. Most of your habits were acquired unintentionally. For example, you decide to try a cigarette. Soon, you're smoking five a day, then ten, and finally two packs. Smoking has then become a habit you acquired unintentionally. Once a habit has been formed, it starts controlling your life. If it's a good habit, that is what you want, and if it's a bad one, it can begin to destroy you. Examples of habits that control us are being optimistic or pessimistic, working hard or being lazy, being punctual or tardy, being tidy or sloppy, and being an early or late riser. To acquire a habit intentionally requires determination and practice. Social scientists tell us it takes about thirty days to acquire or change a habit. When learning the habit of "Allow Time," I would write those words down several times a day, place them on my refrigerator, on the bathroom mirror, and in my office. Forcing me to think about what I wanted to learn sped up the process and helped me develop the necessary discipline. By using this method, you can develop the habits that will work to your benefit.

The awesome news is that, once you acquire a habit, you don't have to think about it much any more. You don't say to yourself *it's time to blink my eyes* or *it's time to breathe*. The same is true for habits. You don't have to think *smile*; you just smile. It takes effort to acquire the habits you want, but once you have them, they're yours for keeps.

My mission in this chapter is to introduce you to the habits that will lead to your success and point **You're going to keep getting it until you get it!** out the ones that can harm you. Your assignment is to select the habit that will help you the most and begin acquiring it. In time, you can integrate each beneficial habit into your life.

Here's a thought I find profound. Understanding it will speed your growth and save you misery and heartache. It applies to each of life's lessons.

If you don't learn a lesson the first time, you'll keep repeating it until you do. This is why learning lessons the first time you get them is so important:

When you lose, don't lose the lesson.

Let's say you've had too much to drink and still decide to drive. You run a stop sign and get pulled over by a policeman. He doesn't notice you've been drinking and only gives you a warning for running the stop sign. That's what's called a *whispering*. If you understand, you were fortunate and you don't drink and drive again. If you don't hear the whispering, you soon make the same mistake again. The next time you're not as lucky and you get written up and lose your license. That's a bigger whispering. If you still don't learn your lesson and you drink and drive, your next whispering may be from your jail cell. You will repeat the lessons until you learn them, and with each repetition, the consequences are usually more severe. This especially applies to life's vices like lying, overeating, gambling, infidelity, cheating, and every other action that gets us into trouble.

Now, let's examine the good habits you can acquire that will help you thrive and flourish.

LOVE

Love is conceivably the most important word in any language. Let's begin by looking at the habit of love. In *The Greatest Salesman*, Og Mandino said:

> *"If you have no other qualities you can succeed with love alone and without it you will fail though you possess all the knowledge and skills of the world."*

That's a commanding statement and should be motivation enough for you to acquire the habit of love. Perhaps this is the best definition of love:

> *Giving of one's self without thought of anything in return*

It follows that love requires unselfish acts. Thinking of love in those terms makes it easier to understand why it's such a powerful emotion. When you see a person do something for another and know he or she's not seeking anything in return, it touches you in a deep and lasting way. We are defenseless against that kind of love. You experience it watching a mother caring for her baby, a child playing with a dog, a husband putting his wife's needs before his own, or siblings guarding each other's back. We live in a culture in which the central concern seems to be *what's in it for me?* Focus on self leads you to the place where disappointment and suffering reside. When you focus on others, you're headed to the land of joy and tranquility. Love will warm the coldest heart. There is no defense for unselfish love. Love's the most essential habit to acquire and that's why I'm introducing it first.

You learned in human relations that *all I give is given to myself.* Therefore, when you give love, you're giving it to yourself. It's intelligent to look upon all things with love, and when you do, it's like experiencing rainbows all day long. Learn to love nature and people regardless of color, nationality, creed, or religion. Develop the habit of love and you'll eliminate the habit of hate, which harms the one carrying it as well as the one it's directed toward. Resentment, slander, and envy are all forms of hatred and are to be eliminated.

Please reconsider the Golden Rule: *Do unto others as you would have others do unto you.* Perhaps a more appropriate rule is: *Do unto others as they would have you do unto them.*

We're all different so it's frequently unwise to treat others the way you want to be treated, but it's always wise to treat others the way they want to be treated. Consider these examples: you like lamb and have a secret best-ever recipe and you want to surprise your best friends with a wonderful dinner. At mealtime, however, you discover they don't eat lamb. Or maybe you love drama and decide to throw your friend a surprise party for her twenty-first birthday. But your friend does not like large gatherings and hates being the center of attention. I could go on, but you can already see that the real secret is to treat people the way they want to be treated.

While acquiring the habit of love, you'll learn the formula for acquiring other things you want. Commence by breaking your goal down into manageable pieces by practicing this principle:

Small efforts repeated will complete any task.

No matter how high the mountain, you can only climb one step at a time. Regardless of how many pages the book needs to have, you can only write it one word at a time. You can only swim a river one stroke at a time. Using this approach to the things you wish to accomplish means they don't seem overwhelming. Given that love is giving of yourself without requiring anything in return, let's consider some ways to practice love:

1. Give of your time. You can cheer up patients at a children's hospital, read to the residents of a home for the elderly, serve the needy at Thanksgiving, or coach a Little League team. You'll be surprised at how great you feel about yourself when you make it a practice to serve others.

2. You can practice love by making people feel important. Give them smiles and compliments, show them appreciation and approval, and let them go and be first.

3. You are practicing love when you give up your seat to an elderly person or help him or her carry packages or cross a street.

4. Buying a lunch or dinner for the person sitting alone in the restaurant where you're eating is a gratifying way to practice love. My wife is a big proponent of this act and I've been amazed at the responses of people when they find you've blessed them without knowing them.

Through these unselfish acts, you'll feel great about yourself and the people you're kind to may offer similar generosity to others, who may in turn pass the good act along. Practice doing unselfish acts and you'll soon attain the habit of love.

SELF-RESPONSIBILITY

This habit is one you must acquire to have peace of mind. You may think you already accept responsibility for your life and I hope that's true, but if it is, you're as rare as a snowstorm in Las Vegas. Let's take a careful look at what accepting responsibility is and see how you measure up. Accepting responsibility means you don't blame anyone else for your problems. It means the buck stops with you. You don't find yourself complaining that your tribulations are anyone else's fault. You don't whine or complain that someone else is making your life miserable or uncomfortable. You never say things like "If my boss didn't make me work the early shift, I wouldn't have come in late," because you know that no matter what shift you work it's your duty to be on time. You don't use the alibi that your bad temper is in your genes because your dad had one, because you grasp that your disposition is solely your responsibility. You don't excuse your awful moods by blaming your boyfriend's lack of thoughtfulness because you realize his actions are up to him and your moods are up to you. Once you've accepted and developed the habit of self-responsibility, there's no longer anyone to point the finger at or to blame. If you don't like something, you change it and you don't look to anyone else to solve your problems. Next time you feel aggravated by a person or circumstance, keep in mind that you're not reacting to the person or the condition but to your own feelings. Your feelings are in your control. Once you have a handle on this concept, you'll take responsibility for how you feel, and if you don't like something, you'll simply change it. As you develop self-responsibility, your life will improve. You'll feel a renewed sense of satisfaction and power knowing that no matter what's wrong, you can correct it.

The following true story illustrates this concept of self-responsibility. Several years ago, a young woman was invited to attend an address by an important speaker at a small college. The auditorium was filled with students excited about the opportunity to hear a person of the speaker's stature. After the introduction, the speaker moved to the microphone, surveyed the audience, and began: "I was born to a mother who was deaf and could not speak. I don't know who my father is or was. The first job I had was in a cotton field." The audience was spellbound. "Nothing has to remain the way it is if that's not the way a person wants it to be," she continued. "It isn't luck, and it isn't circumstances, and it isn't being born a certain way that causes a person's future to become what it becomes." And she softly repeated:

> *"Nothing has to remain the way it is if that's not the way a person wants it to be. All a person has to do to change a situation that brings unhappiness or dissatisfaction is answer the following question: what do I want this situation to become? Then the person must commit totally to personal actions that carry them there."*

Then with a beautiful smile, she said, "My name is Azie Taylor Morton. I stand before you today as treasurer of the United States of America."

You'll notice she didn't say you have to figure out whose fault the problem is or who to blame. Accept full responsibility for every aspect of your life from this day forward. Don't blame anyone for something you don't like about your life. Just follow the wise words of Azie Taylor Morton and figure out how you want it to be and then commit to personal action and make it happen.

SELF-DISCIPLINE

Anyone who wants to travel the road of wisdom, success, and happiness must first travel the road of self-discipline. Rigorous self-discipline and consideration for others are the behaviors of an enlightened person. Self-discipline is a prerequisite to success and happiness. Self-discipline means *doing what you should when you don't feel like doing it.* It's doing what you recognize you should do to get the things you want. To the impatient person, discipline is exasperating. You won't become master of anything until you become master of yourself. When you surrender to a bad habit for the pleasure it brings, you forfeit the right to rule yourself.

Self-discipline is giving yourself a command and then carrying it out.

The people who can do this are on their way to an amazing life; those who can't are condemned to mediocrity. There are many examples of self-discipline, such as telling yourself, "Starting tomorrow, I will rise daily at six in the morning," and then doing it, or saying, "In order to control my weight, I'll limit myself to one portion at mealtimes," and then sticking to it. Every time you give yourself a command and carry it out, you have practiced self-discipline and made yourself stronger. Keeping your word to yourself is crucial in your quest for self-discipline. The habit of self-discipline is the underpinning of making your life turn out the way you want. Self-indulgence in any form is followed by unhappiness. Self-discipline is followed by peace. The person with self-discipline sets a course for each aspect of his or her life and then follows it.

Let's look at some examples of the two sides of the self-discipline coin. Why was the television evangelist caught on tape with a prostitute? How did a man eat enough to weigh 800 pounds? Why are so many celebrities arrested for drunk driving? What caused the CEO to commit fraud? Why did the college student flunk out of the first semester? In each case, the predicament came from a lack of self-discipline. In high school, the parents and teachers provide the discipline, but in college, the student must develop it or fail. Conversely, we observe the athletes who set world records while still in their teens, the formerly homeless person who graduates from Harvard, the janitor who leaves $100,000 to charity, and Tiger Woods, who has rewritten the record books.

This is one of my favorite sayings:

A little thing is a little thing, but faithfulness in little things is a big thing.

All big things are only a series of little things. Whether it's the Empire State Building, the Eiffel Tower, a Boeing 777, or the city of San Francisco, each of these big things is simply a series of little things put together. That's the way for you to look at self-discipline. If you don't have it, the way to get it is through repeated small attempts.

The weak become strong by attaching importance to little things and then doing them devotedly.

You can commence by disciplining yourself to rise early every day. If you give yourself that command and do it for thirty days in a row, you'll acquire the habit and also gain knowledge of the benefits of self-discipline. After that, you may want to gain control of your eating, then moderate your drinking, and then enhance your smiling. Each time you gain a new discipline, you're improving your supply of good habits and with each one your life will improve. You will inevitably learn to live by principle and not passion. Once you acquire self-discipline, you'll leave the dusty dirt road of life with all its potholes and bumps and enter a smooth freeway, which will allow you to speed down the path to success and happiness.

QUIZ — HOW SELF-DISCIPLINED ARE YOU?

1 When you watch your favorite TV show, you usually keep watching a few more shows, even if you don't really like them all that much.

☐ True   ☐ False

2 When you're late for meeting someone, you feel guilty, even if you've let them know.

☐ True   ☐ False

3 You'll do whatever it takes to do what you're supposed to do—for school or work or for a friend—no matter what you have to sacrifice.

☐ True   ☐ False

4 You are determined to exercise—if you have the time and other things don't get in the way.

☐ True   ☐ False

5 You're the kind of person who likes making lists so you can check things off when they're done.

☐ True   ☐ False

SCORE	Count up your points, then flip to the end of the chapter to find out what your score means.

1. True - 0 points; False - 5
2. True - 5 points; False - 0
3. True - 5 points; False - 0
4. True - 0 points; False - 5
5. True - 5 points; False - 0

INDUSTRIOUSNESS

Laziness is one of the universal causes of failure. All forms of procrastination are laziness. Shirking and neglecting responsibilities is laziness. Do you know why some people are successful? *Because they're willing to do the things unsuccessful people are not willing to do.*

The first step to achieving your goals is desire and the stronger your desire, the more industrious you become. Even when you have desire, it's only effective when it's crystallized into resolve. The stronger your desire and resolve, the more willing you'll be to meet the demands necessary for your success. When your desires are strong enough, you'll value time and not waste it. If you lack motivation and you want to acquire the habit of industriousness, the first step is to amplify your desire. When you develop a burning desire about the things you want, industriousness will follow.

The formula is the same to acquire any habit you want. Identify the habit, write it down, and place it where you see it often, then practice it repeatedly until it becomes yours.

Examples of industriousness include becoming more meticulous, learning more about your profession, and practicing self-improvement.

TAKING ACTION

No matter how intense your desire or how smart you may be, there's no hope of achieving victory unless you act. Your dreams and plans are empty until you take action. Thinking is good, but thinking alone can't make anything happen.

A wish or hope is merely a desire with no effort to accomplish it.

No mouth can be fed or dollar earned without action. Wishing and hoping can't create success.

Nothing worthwhile can happen without action. The following anecdote is a painful personal example of the importance of action. You may recall the dotcom boom in the late '90s. Companies were going public at a record pace and stockholders were making fortunes. There were many new Internet startups, such as Amazon, eBay and E-Trade. Many if not most of them weren't profitable; however, their stock prices continued soaring. I'd invested in a company called LookSmart. I purchased 10,000 shares at $2.00 a share before the company went public. After the IPO, the stock was selling for $70 per share. My $20,000 investment was worth $700,000. I decided to sell and called my broker. I was informed there was a mandatory waiting period. I was also instructed I'd have to file some paperwork in order to sell. I began thinking the stock would almost certainly keep going up if I held it. I didn't act. Time passed and I continued sitting on the sidelines. One year later, the stock that had been worth $700,000 was now worth $12,000. Because of my inaction, I cost my family $688,000. There are two significant messages here:

Make thoughtful decisions and make them promptly.

To act and fail is better than not to act and flounder. It's better to regret something you did than something you didn't do. Action is the habit of successful people. Nothing should be put off that needs to be done.

QUIZ   HOW RATIONAL OR IMPULSIVE ARE YOU?

1 Do you like surprises?

- **a** Yes.
- **b** Yes, as long as they're good ones.
- **c** No.

2 Have you ever cheated to get a better grade?

- **a** Yes, but it was really important to pull my overall average up.
- **b** Yes, but I felt so bad I would never do it again.
- **c** No, it's just not worth it.

3 When you go to the store because you have run out of something you need . . .

- **a** I come back with a few other things as well.
- **b** I buy that item and others that I forgot to put on the list.
- **c** I get just that item and come home.

4 How do you feel about puzzles that have more than fifty pieces to fit together?

- **a** Boring! I'd rather watch paint dry than do a puzzle.
- **b** If I were on a desert island and that were the only thing to do, then I'd do it.
- **c** I think they seem geeky but I secretly like them.

QUIZ	HOW RATIONAL OR IMPULSIVE ARE YOU? *(continued)*

5 If you were having trouble in the dating area, what would you do?

    a Just go to a lot more parties and hope I might meet someone.

    b Ask friends if they know anyone right for me.

    c Go on the Internet to get some tips.

SCORE	Count up the number of times you answered a, b, and c, then flip to the end of the chapter to find out what your score means.

PATIENCE

Nature doesn't act in haste and because we are part of nature, neither should we. Patience isn't embraced by many in the under-thirty generation, where people want everything immediately. There's a good rationale for the old saying "Patience is a virtue." Trees, companies, wisdom, and babies grow slowly. It takes time to learn or build anything worthwhile. Most overnight successes actually take about fifteen years. Consider the time necessary to learn to play a musical instrument,

Those who are patient can have what they will.

make the dean's list, become a doctor, be a proficient golfer, or develop a real friendship. Acquiring worthwhile things takes time and requires patience. Patience makes discipline beautiful.

Pacing yourself and allowing time will bring you success and peace of mind.

Your impatience may annoy others, but it hurts, wounds, and impoverishes you the most.

I became a racecar driver at age forty-nine and learned I occasionally needed to slow down to go faster. When you approach a turn, there's an optimum speed to get through the corner. If you exceed that speed, you won't pass through

Sometimes you need to slow down to go faster.

the corner as fast as a driver who's going slower but at the optimum speed. The car going too fast will slide sideways, losing time. Given that this is true in a racecar, it makes sense that it applies to other aspects of life. There was a reason the tortoise beat the hare. Slow and steady usually wins the race.

Today, too many seem to be going too fast. They eat, read, shop, talk, drive, and generally do everything too fast. You can save yourself much pain and heartache while you're still young if you learn patience. It's a rare virtue and immediately sets you apart from the ordinary. It's comforting to know you can have whatever you want if you are willing to be patient and work toward it steadily. One way to become a standout is to slow down and work with precision. Meticulousness can mean the difference between a life of peace and power and one of misery and weakness. Excellence will always be in demand and it requires patience.

QUIZ   **HOW PATIENT ARE YOU?**

1 I would say I feel stressed out . . .

   a Daily.
   b Several times a week.
   c Once a week or less.

2 When I'm in a tense situation, the first thing I do is . . .

   a Freak out and lose it.
   b Feel like crying but suck it up.
   c Try to catch my breath.

3 After a stressful situation, I usually feel . . .

   a Guilty and ashamed.
   b Tired and still not in control.
   c Relieved it's over.

4 When I feel like I'm ready to freak out, I usually . . .

- **a** Am tempted to go out partying.
- **b** Pig out.
- **c** Hit the gym really hard.

5 In my family, when my parents get really stressed, they . . .

- **a** Yell and argue.
- **b** Try to keep things calm by not talking about it.
- **c** Yell at first, but then try to talk it over later.

6 The thing that really makes me lose my temper is . . .

- **a** When I feel like someone is insulting me or not listening to me.
- **b** When I feel as if I did something stupid.
- **c** When I get hurt physically or am in pain.

7 I think I could be calmer and less frustrated most of the time if I . . .

- **a** Felt as if my life was going better than it is now.
- **b** Had more friends who accepted me for who I am, even when I mess up.
- **c** Could talk to other people about how I felt before things get out of hand.

QUIZ	**HOW PATIENT ARE YOU?** *(continued)*

8 When I lose my temper with someone I wail on them . . .

- **a** Often.
- **b** Sometimes.
- **c** Never.

9 The one thing I wish I could do when I lose my patience is . . .

- **a** Just go to sleep until it passes.
- **b** Walk away before I say things I'll regret.
- **c** Figure out how stay calm.

10 If a friend promises to call and doesn't . . .

- **a** It drives me nuts.
- **b** The next day when I see him or her I'll be honest about how upset I am.
- **c** I'll pick up the phone and call him or her.

SCORE Count up the number of times you answered a, b, and c, then flip to the end of the chapter to find out what your score means.

PERSISTENCE

A lack of persistence is a universal reason for failure. Knowing exactly what you want is the first step to acquiring persistence. Determination combined with a burning desire will lead you to persistence. Weak desires lead to weak results. Our principle of small repeated attempts completing any task applies here. When you break large goals down into smaller ones, they become easier to accomplish. As you meet your smaller goals, the bigger ones become less formidable. Let's use the example of running a marathon: when you imagine running twenty-six miles at one stretch, it seems a daunting task. When you first begin to train, you feel enthusiasm and excitement, but before long the adventure becomes less appealing. It soon becomes a grind and seems it will take forever. Your feet and legs ache and the weather doesn't cooperate. Your practice runs begin taking up all your spare time. This is when your test begins. Quitting is easy and can become a bad habit. Your marathon quest starts by being able to run one mile. Your next goal is running five miles. You don't think about the twenty-six-mile run but remain focused on the shorter distances. Once you can run five miles, you move on to ten, then fifteen, then twenty, and finally you accomplish your goal of twenty-six miles. By breaking your goal down into manageable pieces, you're more apt to persist and your commitment increases with the more time and effort you put into any project. Keep in mind that a flood starts with a few drops of rain, a forest fire begins with one small spark, and a hurricane commences from a breeze. It's the accomplishment of our small goals that allows us to complete our big ones.

An important step to help you learn persistence is establishing a compelling *Why.* If you're running a marathon to honor your child who's fighting cancer, you have a much better chance of succeeding than the person who simply thinks it would be fun. The bigger the *Why* you have for doing anything, the better the odds that you'll persist. When you begin your next challenge, write out all the reasons *why* you want to accomplish it, and when the going gets tough, refer to your list.

The rewards for the things we want to accomplish are generally at the end of the task, not near the beginning. If you decide to learn a foreign language, it's rough sledding at first. You can't pronounce the words, you don't understand the grammar, and you can't even form a simple sentence. It takes several months before it's any fun, but persistence pays big dividends and it takes self-discipline to develop persistence.

You never know exactly when success will arrive, so you have to keep moving forward until you get what you want. There's a true story of a gold miner who worked his mine for five years and found little gold. He became frustrated and decided to quit and sold his mine to the first person who made him an offer. The new owner started digging and, after digging only three feet, discovered one of the largest veins of gold in Nevada history. Oh, what a little more persistence would have meant to the quitter. I like the way Winston Churchill put it: "Never give up. Never ever give up."

HUMILITY

Humility is one of the most underrated habits. Some people even think of it as a weakness. Nothing could be further from the truth.

Humility distinguishes the thoughtful person from the person focused on self. The humble person thinks and speaks of the absent person tenderly and respectfully. The opposite of humility is arrogance and any form of arrogance is repulsive and dangerous. We display humility by being respectful, patient, encouraging, and non-

Humility is not putting oneself above others or being prideful.

prideful, and by keeping the spotlight on others. We display arrogance when we focus attention on ourselves, brag, put people down, insist on our own way, or lord it over others. The humble person is quick to admit mistakes or that he or she may be wrong.

The true story that follows demonstrates the serious consequences of a lack of humility. My mentor was celebrating his fiftieth wedding anniversary at a local restaurant. There were ten of us, including his son, his accountant, his attorney, me, and all our wives. My mentor had included me in his will with a life estate and had done the same for his attorney and his son. At the dinner, my wife and I had been seated next to my mentor and his wife while the attorney and his wife had been seated at the far end of the table. The day after the celebration, at a business meeting, the attorney commented that his wife had complained about the seating arrangement, wondering why he and his wife had been seated at the far end of the table. I'll never forget the look on my mentor's face when asked this question. He paused for several seconds and then said, "I had my reasons." That was the end of the discussion; we concluded our business and the attorney left. Then my mentor told me why he had seated this man and his wife where he did. But before I recount what he said, I want to let you know the consequences of his question. The attorney was dismissed. He was taken out of my mentor's will and lost his share of the life estate. Asking that question cost the attorney more than one million dollars and a relationship with the wisest and most generous man I've ever known. All of these consequences were the result of a lack of humility. The reason he and his wife had been seated at the far end of the table was because she smoked. No matter where they had been seated, the prudent person would have been thankful to be invited and left it at that. Even if his wife felt slighted, it was arrogant to air this complaint. Just think of losing one million dollars because of arrogance and it will help you acquire the wonderful virtue and habit of humility.

DECISIVENESS

This is an essential habit of most successful people. Once you evaluate the facts, it's important to make a decision and then be slow to change your mind. Decisiveness is like a razor-sharp knife that cuts cleanly and quickly, while indecision is like a dull knife that tears and rips as it tries to cut. How often do we hear people say, "I just can't make up my mind"? This makes dealing with them difficult. Indecision is the seedling of fear and is caused by doubt. It's a sign of confidence to be decisive and displaying confidence breeds confidence. If you're indecisive, someone else will grab the gold ring while you're mulling things over. To learn decisiveness, you must practice it. A good place to start is when placing your order in a restaurant, picking out new clothes, selecting a movie to watch, or deciding where to go on vacation. Decisiveness requires keeping your eyes on the road ahead once you make a decision. Indecisive people tend to keep one eye in the rearview mirror. Get out of the habit of looking back if you want to become decisive. Once you make a decision, consider it water under the bridge. Eliminate worry, doubt, and fear concerning anything that is in the past. Your future lies ahead of you, not behind. Don't be the person who orders the shrimp and then sits at the table wondering if the lasagna would have been a better choice. Don't second-guess yourself. Let your *yes* be *yes* and your *no* be *no*. Get in the habit of thinking things through carefully, then making a decision and sticking to it.

MASTERING YOUR EMOTIONS

This habit leads to psychological health and calmness. Losing control of your emotions usually causes pain and impairs your ability to practice good human relations. When you lose control, your blood pressure rises, your confidence declines, and worst of all, you often overreact. It's a time when you can say and do things you will later regret.

Learning not to react takes practice but is worth the effort. Moods and emotions are relatives. When we control our emotions, we retain a much better mood. People with large and frequent mood swings are hard to be around. Once you learn to control your own emotions, you'll gain the necessary knowledge to deal effectively with the moods and emotions of others.

If you don't react, you'll never overreact.

To understand emotions, let's begin by looking at the way nature operates. All life moves in cycles. The sun comes up and then goes down, an animal is born and then passes, a plant blooms and a plant dies, the tide comes in and then goes out. Because we're a part of nature, our moods follow this same pattern. Today's bliss will turn into tomorrow's grief and today's sorrow will become tomorrow's happiness. It's helpful to realize that if we're healthy, we're not stuck in one part of the cycle very long. We frequently don't know why we're in a particular mood, but at least we understand the pattern. When you're feeling on top of the world and that life can't get any better, it's wise to enjoy the moment and realize it will pass. When you're down in the dumps and feeling things will never improve, it's important to remind yourself that today's sorrow will pass on to tomorrow's happiness. Once you begin watching your emotions and moods, you'll begin to understand and accept the pattern. Take control of your emotions by becoming more aware of your highs and lows.

Recognize that ups and downs are a natural part of life.

When you're feeling too high or low, bring yourself back to center by recalling the cycle.

How concerned are you today about the problem that seemed so big five years ago? Knowing how your moods work will allow you to apply the same thinking to others. When you see someone flying too high, you'll know they soon will be coming back to earth. When you're around someone in a bad mood, you'll understand that tomorrow he or she may feel happier than ever and be easy to approach. Everyone has ups and downs; however, only a few understand the cycle and how to manage it. As Benjamin Franklin wisely said, "No morning sun lasts a whole day." When things are good or bad, we often think they will remain that way. Now you know that is not true. You may

Take comfort in the fact that no matter what your situation is, it will pass.

experience a drought, but the rain will come again. It's much easier to survive the harsh times when you know happiness is right around the corner.

GENEROSITY

The intention of generosity is to create happiness for the giver and receiver. Generosity is rare and when something is rare, opportunity is frequently knocking.

The old saying about *give and it will be given back to you multiplied many times* is true. I was pleasantly surprised when I began experimenting with generosity. I was working for a real estate firm in San Francisco. When I got paid after closing my first deal, I spent a few dollars on flowers and candy for the administrative people who processed the check. They said it was the first time they'd been given a gift for just doing their job. After that one generous act, they did many kind and accommodating things for me. This encouraged me to become more generous. It's important to realize that doing generous acts is its own reward, whether anything comes back to you or not. There is great joy in the act of giving. Even though many of the principles taught in this book bring direct benefits to you,

A seldom-practiced virtue is an opportunity to set ourselves apart.

the overriding reason to do them is they are the right thing to do, they make others feel better, and they make you feel good about yourself.

The best example I can offer of the power of generosity came when I started my own real estate firm in San José. The standard commission split was 50 percent to the company and 50 percent to the salesperson. I decided to offer our salespeople an 80/20 split with 80 percent going to the salesperson. I thought that would help us attract the best people and that they would remain loyal. We were also one of the few firms to offer our salespeople private offices. Most of our competitors kept their salespeople in a bullpen arrangement. Over time, we became the second-largest commercial real estate firm in Silicon Valley, attracted the best brokers, and few of them ever left. Thirty years later, the firm still holds that commanding position. I attribute much of our success to generosity. Our firm made it a practice to give a gift to each client with whom we closed a transaction. That was unusual and had an amazing effect. Our clients were loyal; we had repeat business and consistent referrals. Our gifts ranged from a bottle of fine wine to grandfather clocks or to a trip to Scotland for golf.

It's often the little acts of generosity that have the most impact on both the giver and receiver. A good way to initiate the practice of generosity is forming the habit of giving something to everyone you come in contact with, even if it is simply a smile or nod of approval. Generosity comes in many forms, including your time, praise, appreciation, and a supportive ear. The most powerful gifts are not material. They include love, caring, attention, affection, and appreciation. Little kindnesses lead to a kind and generous character, which leads to peace and happiness.

GRATITUDE

I'm baffled at the lack of thankfulness and gratitude in our society. We live in a world filled with people who seem to think others owe them something. It feels like we have succumbed to an entitlement mentality.

You should show appreciation for the smallest kindness anyone shows you.

Common sense dictates that you should be grateful to someone who opens doors for you, buys you lunch, says a kind word, remembers your special days, gives you a gift, or looks out for your welfare. Each of these actions is an opportunity to practice gratitude. Gratitude should come from the heart with no ulterior motive. If you don't show gratitude, don't expect people to repeat the kind act. We all need to adopt an attitude of gratitude. Here's a powerful reason to commence the habit of gratitude:

> *It's impossible to feel bad when you're feeling thankful.*

STAYING PRESENT

I used to tell our salespeople that all they had to be was a little above average to be a star. I feel that's even truer today than it was then. People are moving too fast, are too self-centered, and are not paying attention to detail. You see evidence of this by the way people respond when you send them a message. They read the message so quickly that they frequently register only part of what you say. You write something simple like: "Let's have lunch next Thursday at noon" and the reply comes back: "I'm good with lunch. What day would you like to do it?" What that response tells us is they're not staying present. How often have you been talking to someone and in the middle of the conversation he or she stops you and asks what you just said or you see him or her looking away and waving at someone in the distance? That means the person wasn't there while you were talking. The person's body was present, but his or her mind was absent.

This is not the way to win someone's confidence or affection. Let's evaluate how staying present benefits you. To the best of my knowledge, there are only three places the mind can go. It can go to the past, stay in the present, or look to the future. In examining these alternatives individually, a clear picture unfolds. What can happen in

When you don't stay present, you make others feel unimportant.

the past? The answer is nothing. Can you take back something you said or did yesterday? Can you do something you want to do yesterday? Nothing can happen yesterday. Lamenting something that happened yesterday is foolish. It makes sense to reflect on yesterday's mistakes so you don't repeat them. Remembering wonderful people or events from yesterday may be rewarding, but in terms of getting anything done, yesterday doesn't work and neither does tomorrow. Who can say for certain they will even have a tomorrow? Even if you are here tomorrow, that doesn't accomplish anything today. Tomorrow is a day for the lazy who don't want to do what needs doing now. Tomorrow is the resting place for those who live on "Someday Isle." *Someday* I'll get my dream job, find my perfect mate, or clean the garage. *Someday*

I'll set my goals, get my weight under control, or take that trip.

If yesterday is gone and tomorrow may never come, where does that leave us? In the present—and that's the only place anything can happen. On that basis, why on earth would you want to be anywhere else? Logically, there can be no reason except the bad habit of trying to live in the past or future. People allow their minds to wander and their focus to drift. You're having a cup of coffee with a friend, but you find yourself thinking about the exam you must take in two hours. Bring your attention back to the present. Your girlfriend is talking to you about making the cheerleading squad and you're thinking about the golf game you just played. Bring your attention back to the present. As your awareness grows, you'll start staying present and your life will improve.

There are many benefits to staying present.

1. It's the only place you can make anything happen.
2. You're dealing with reality because there is no tomorrow or yesterday right now.
3. When you stay present, those around you feel important.

④ Your life will become more exciting, colorful, and rich as your awareness grows.

⑤ You'll rid yourself of anxiety, worry, doubt, regrets, and fear because rarely do any of those crippling emotions live in the present. Those unsavory characters live in the past or the future.

⑥ There are few problems in the present. You worry about a future that may or may not ever happen. Planning for the future is important, but you can't live there now.

Learn to accept whatever the present moment contains and work with it, not against it. If you find yourself complaining, you are not accepting what is. Stress is not caused by being here but by wanting to be somewhere else. Learn to stay present and watch your life transform.

PUNCTUALITY

Being on time sends a significant message. Whether it's lunch with a friend, picking up your brother or sister from soccer practice, taking your girlfriend on a date, or attending a debate, timeliness shows the person you're meeting that he or she's important to you. It's common for people to arrive for commitments from five to twenty minutes late and think nothing of it. Frequently, they consider it fashionable to turn up late for social gatherings. It's neither fine nor fashionable to be late unless your goal is showing the person you're meeting that he or she is not as important as you.

How does it make you feel when someone keeps you waiting? When a doctor keeps you sitting in the waiting room beyond your appointed time, don't you feel a lack of respect? How good does it make you feel when you walk into the doctor's office on time and the receptionist greets you

If you want to make a good impression, be punctual.

with a big smile and says, "The doctor will see you now." The reason I'm using doctors for my example is because the public largely accepts their lateness. We may put up with it, but we don't feel good about it, and when we find a doctor who is punctual, we have a propensity to stay with him or her. Make it your practice to be a person others can set their watches by. The rewards will be immense.

You learn to be on time by making it a priority and then a habit. The secret is to *allow time*. Things don't always go perfectly, and even if they do, running in at the last second is not good for your nervous system. I worked hard to acquire the habit of allowing time and it has served me well for decades. People appreciate knowing they can depend on the fact I won't keep them waiting. My friends tell me they arrive early when meeting with me because they know I'll be there waiting. It's an excellent reputation to have because it shows respect.

To acquire the habit of punctuality, I suggest you learn to use Lombardi time. Vince Lombardi was the famous coach who took control of the Green Bay Packers in 1959. They were a hopeless team at the time and he led them to five world championships in the following nine years. His rule for his players was this: *if you're not fifteen minutes early, you're late.* We adopted Lombardi time at our real estate firm and it proved beneficial. Put yourself on Lombardi time and you'll have less stress, lower blood pressure, and a wonderful reputation for making others feel important. If you think it's going to take you fifteen minutes to get somewhere, allow thirty. It's a great feeling to be early for an appointment and it allows you the luxury of relaxing your mind and body before your meeting.

SAVING

I hope you already have this habit. It troubles me to see a seventy-year-old woman working as a housecleaner because she doesn't have enough money to retire. I feel the same for the elderly man who's busing tables at night. It's even worse to see the men and women living on the streets. To be sure you avoid suffering this fate, acquire the habit of saving. Too many young people think they can worry about saving when they get older. Saving is a habit and the sooner you develop this habit the sooner you'll have money working for you while you work for money. Money can multiply surprisingly fast if put to good use. When money works, it does not eat, drink, or sleep, and it's on the job every day of the year, with no vacation.

Here's an example of the way money can multiply. Say you begin saving and investing when you graduate from high school at age seventeen. For the first five years, you save $200 a month. At the end of five years, using a seven percent rate of return (interest rates have varied in my life from 1% to 15%), you'll have $14,178. At twenty-two, you increase your savings to $500 a month for eight years. At age thirty, your account will be $78,008. Then you increase to $800 a month for the next ten years. At age forty, your account is $314,431. As you hit your stride in business, you increase your savings to $1,000 a month until you're fifty. At fifty, you'll have $732,242. You can see that by the time you're sixty you'll have amassed more than $1,000,000. You won't be a seventy-year-old forced to do a minimum wage job to survive. Your million dollars will be in addition to any job-related retirement plan, plus your social security income.

It's not how much money you make; it's how much you keep.

Indiscriminate spending is one of the greatest causes of failure. The spendthrift will not succeed financially. Money in the bank gives you courage and allows you to make rational decisions. The sooner you get the savings habit and get your money working for you, the better your future will become.

MANNERS AND GRACES

The purpose of manners and graces is to open up social situations for you. An added bonus is the fact you feel good about yourself when you use them. Without good manners, no matter how brilliant you may be you won't win with people. Good manners are like a beautiful painting that makes people feel good when they are around it. Bad manners are like a dirty rag that no one wants to look at or touch. Good manners open doors for you, impress those with whom you associate, and provide opportunities for you that are not available to those without them. Consider the way you feel when you're talking and get interrupted. How about when you're dining with someone and she talks with food in her mouth? How do you feel when you're around someone who contradicts his wife or cuts in line, has bad breath, food in his teeth, or is wearing dirty and wrinkled clothes? Each of these situations is repellent rather than attractive.

Now let's take a look at the actions that constitute good manners and graces and make sure they are the actions you adopt:

1. Let others go first whether it be talking, going through doors, sitting down, or ordering.
2. Keep your speech civil, using no vulgarity.
3. Eliminate gossip and practice praise.
4. Smile when you greet someone.
5. Eat slowly, don't talk with food in your mouth, keep your elbows off the table, and use your napkin.
6. Don't slurp when you drink.
7. Don't contradict.
8. Always say *please* and *thank you.*
9. Get permission before using anything that does not belong to you.
10. Always be on time.

(11) Call older people Mr. and Ms. until invited to do otherwise.

(12) Say you're sorry if you do something wrong and be quick to admit mistakes.

(13) Pick up after yourself.

(14) Help with the cleanup when you're a guest.

(15) Bring a small gift when invited to someone's home.

(16) Send a handwritten thank-you note when someone does something nice for you.

(17) Stand when a lady enters the room and always stand up to shake hands.

(18) Return messages promptly and carry out tasks you agree to do as soon as possible.

(19) Make the bed if you're the last one out of it.

(20) Always do what you say you will do.

(21) Speak softly.

(22) Don't answer your cell phone or respond to a text message when meeting with anyone.

(23) Don't play your music so loud it disturbs others.

(24) Eliminate sarcasm.

REGRETS

It's extremely important when you're young to understand the foolishness of dwelling on regrets. No good can come of it and it will diminish your self-esteem as well as your confidence. It's impossible to go through life without doing things we're sorry we did. One of the ways we gain knowledge is by doing things that don't turn out the way we hope they will. The key is learning from your mistakes and not repeating them.

When you lose, don't lose the lesson.

Confine your thinking to the road ahead and keep your eyes off the rearview mirror. The past is over and there is nothing you can do about it now. Regrets cannot help your future, so eliminate them.

TURNING POINTS

As you travel the pathway of life, you're going to have opportunities that can dramatically influence your future. My wife had one of those experiences several years ago when some friends invited her to scale Half Dome in Yosemite National Park. She's not a powerfully built person and had never done anything requiring that kind of stamina. The climb started at five in the morning and took more than twelve hours to complete. It involved climbing up a trail to reach the face, climbing the face, and then the trip all the way back down. Several of the participants who appeared much more athletic than my wife were not able to complete the circuit. To this day, she tells me she's never experienced anything as difficult and how proud she was to finish the climb. Her confidence is higher because of completing this challenge and she now feels she can complete whatever comes her way.

I have witnessed the same kind of turning points here on the Big Island with the participants who complete the Ironman Triathlon. It's hard to imagine even attempting it. It takes the best athletes in the world in the neighborhood of seven hours to finish. Those who complete it claim it changes their lives by giving them confidence for other trials they face. The same can be said for those who complete a marathon. The point is that you'll have your own life-altering opportunity, and when it comes, seize it. Don't let fear hold you back from any of your dreams. The turtle doesn't get anywhere unless it sticks its neck out and you can't steal second base while keeping one foot on first. *Carpe diem*—seize the day.

HABITS TO AVOID

Being aware of your bad habits will help you avoid them. If you have any of the following bad habits, you'll want to replace them with the opposite good one. This list is not in any particular order—all of these will cause you trouble, misery, and heartache: anger, lust, greed, laziness, sloppiness, deceit, lying, gluttony, hate, vanity, fear, worry, doubt, blame, jealousy, gambling, fault-finding, indecision, impatience, carelessness, complaining, talking too much, exaggerating, intemperance, extravagance, immodesty, criticism, contradiction, entitlement, procrastination, indifference, over-cautiousness, overspending, revenge, superstition, vulgarity, selfishness, intolerance, rigidity, lethargy, promiscuity, disloyalty, envy, and quitting.

CONCLUSION

Habits may not be the most exciting or glamorous subject you've studied, but they are clearly one of the most vital because I'm encouraging you to take this chapter seriously. I recommend you carefully evaluate each habit and select the one you feel will help you the most and begin acquiring it. Allow thirty days to acquire each habit by following the instructions in this chapter. By doing this with each habit and then doing the same for the habits to

Your success or failure will depend on your habits.

avoid, you'll set yourself up for an extraordinary life.

Acting or not acting depends on perspective. Don't be the skeptic who sits on the sidelines and ponders proven principles. Take the perspective that all you just read was written for your betterment. Let the other guy sit and wait for his ship to come in while you swim out to yours. Be the person who can see at a glance what others cannot see with a telescope.

One of the most perplexing things to me is how someone can be given a proven plan that will improve his or her life and then not implement it.

None of what you've read is speculation. Not only have these methods worked for me, they have worked for thousands and for centuries. This is where the saying "You can lead a horse to water but you can't make it drink" comes from. All anyone can do is provide you with the information you need to succeed—then it's up to you to act. If you want triumph beyond your most extravagant dreams, take what you've read literally. Once you implement the instructions, you'll set yourself up for peace, happiness, and prosperity. You can prove the validity of the instructions by starting with one new habit and marveling at the way it enhances your life. Then you can implement the others.

QUIZ ANSWERS

● HOW SELF-DISCIPLINED ARE YOU?

What your score means:

If you scored between 0 and 10 points, are you really trying as hard as you can to take care of business? You might want to try a little harder.

If you scored between 15 and 20 points, good job—you're really working at taking control of your life and reaching your goals.

If you scored more than 25 points, great—you're on your way to succeeding in whatever you try for in life. Keep it up!

● HOW RATIONAL OR IMPULSIVE ARE YOU?

What your score means:

MOSTLY As: You are quite impulsive. You follow your heart more than your head. That can be a good thing, though you might also think about expanding your rational side.

MOSTLY Bs: You are both impulsive and rational—a good combination. If your other answers leaned toward one side or the other, you might want to continue to aim for balance in your actions.

MOSTLY Cs: You tend to follow your head more often than your heart. While this can be a very valuable trait, especially in business, you may want to try listening a little more to your heart for the next few weeks and seeing how it goes.

● HOW PATIENT ARE YOU?

What your score means:

MOSTLY As: You tend to get frustrated pretty easily and you let it out in ways you often regret. You feel as if others don't really get how much pressure you feel and how hard it is to deal with it. You know you shouldn't always do the things you do when stressed. And you're going to try to talk things over first, and to deal with what life throws at you more calmly.

MOSTLY Bs: You work hard at dealing patiently with all the stress in your life, but sometimes you'd just rather walk away and see if it sorts itself out on its own. You know you hide your feelings more than you should. And you plan to work on opening up, so you don't feel so lonely. Then you'll be able to figure out more positive ways to stay calm and feel more in control of your life

MOSTLY Cs: You feel as if you're dealing with the stress in your life pretty well, but even so sometimes you just lose it. You work really hard at being in control; maybe sometimes you try too hard. You know you're pretty calm compared to most of your friends, and people feel they can come to you for help. Still, you want to keep on trying new things to help you feel relaxed and more confident about your life and your future.

3

MAKING YOUR
DREAMS COME TRUE

It was a beautiful spring morning in Fresno, California. A young woman stood at her front door and asked me to come in as I was delivering her milk. She and I had become friendly over the past six months. This day she asked me if I'd be interested in a position at Xerox. She told me her husband managed the local office and that she could arrange an interview for me. I told her I enjoyed the milk business and she said she thought I could do much better. When she revealed how much money her husband made, I was astonished. I thought I was doing well, but compared to him, I was making a pauper's wage. So, in my mid-twenties, I found myself walking into the tallest building in Fresno, headed for the top floor. When the elevator opened,

I saw a spectacular view and offices that were stunning. I'd purchased a black suit, black shoes, and a short-sleeved white shirt from Sears for the interview. I didn't realize how silly my standard milkman white socks looked with black pants and shoes. A tall, handsome man came out and invited me into his office. He was wearing a gray suit with a vest and a long-sleeved white shirt with stylish cuff links. When we were seated, I told him I appreciated his wife arranging the interview. He asked which college I'd attended and I told him I hadn't gone to college. He informed me that Xerox only hired college graduates, so there was no reason to continue the interview. I inquired who Xerox's principal competitor was and he said it was Addressograph-Multigraph Corporation. I went directly to the lobby and placed a call to Addressograph-Multigraph Corporation. I asked to speak with the manager and he was soon on the line. I reviewed what had just taken place with him and informed him that my mission was to begin displacing Xerox equipment. He seemed intrigued and invited me to his office. After interviewing me for an hour, he said I had a job. He instructed me to lose the white socks, and to purchase three new suits with vests and long-sleeved white shirts with French cuffs. In the subsequent eighteen months, I replaced a great deal of Xerox equipment.

One day, out of the blue, I received a surprising phone call. The caller asked if I'd consider working for Xerox. I relayed the story of my interview and informed him that I still didn't have a college education. He told me he'd already discounted that obstacle and that he was prepared to offer me a job. I took the job and enjoyed great success at Xerox. I was soon promoted to sales manager and given my own sales team. I eventually became discontented with the layers of rules and regulations. I'd suggest ideas that were well received, only to find I couldn't implement them because of corporate policy. I realized it was time to move on.

I decided to pursue a career selling whatever product allowed me to make the most money. After reading *The Magic of Thinking Big*, I was determined to put what I'd learned into practice. I uncovered three suitable possibilities: I could sell ships, airplanes, or buildings. With a little more research, I eliminated ships and planes because I would have needed a great deal of technical knowledge in order to sell them. That left me with buildings. The largest buildings in Northern California were in San Francisco, so I began interviewing there for a position in commercial real estate. After securing a position, I got off to an unusually fast start by closing eleven transactions in my first three months. To my surprise, one month later the owner asked if I'd consider opening an office for him in San José. I'd never been to San José, but it seemed a good opportunity, so I agreed. It took three months to close my first transaction in the new area. Business was good after that and I began growing the office. By October 1974, we were doing exceedingly well. I'd hired three new salespeople and established an enviable reputation. My workday was 5:00 A.M. to 6:00 P.M., six days a week. I also went to night school, pursuing my broker's license. Two seasoned salespeople had recently left the firm after ten years of service to start their own companies once they acquired their broker's licenses. This alarmed the owner and made him distrust anyone pursuing a broker's license. Late one Friday afternoon in October 1974, he arrived at my office unannounced and told me that if I didn't drop the idea of a getting a broker's license, I would lose my job. I wasn't one to be threatened or intimidated, so I resigned. I had a sick feeling driving home that night, knowing I was about to tell my family I no longer had a job. The owner proceeded to fire my secretary the same day. The following Monday morning, I started my own company and rehired my secretary.

I've shared this story with you because there are a number of life lessons you can learn from it:

① **You never know who's watching and may help you** as the woman on my milk route proved.

② **When one door closes, you can open another** if you're determined, creative, and have grit and ambition. Xerox closed the door, but that inspired me to seek out their main competitor, which led to my future in sales.

③ **If you don't like the situation you're in, change it.** In my case, it was leaving Xerox and getting into commercial real estate.

④ **The final lesson I want you to recognize is the most important. When something happens to you, don't judge it as good or bad at the time. Wait and see how it turns out.** Being fired for pursuing my broker's license seemed unfair and ruinous at the time, but it turned out to be one of the grand blessings of my life. The success that came to me from starting my own company would never have happened had I not been threatened by my previous employer. I would have gone on to build a successful company for someone else. I wouldn't have made enough money to retire at fifty-five if I hadn't started my own firm. I would not be writing this book to benefit others had I not encountered what seemed a huge setback.

YOU HAVE TO HAVE A DREAM TO MAKE A DREAM COME TRUE

Many important principles appear simple and obvious, yet they're seldom practiced. That's true for the first step to making your dreams of success and happiness come true. When asked if they have dreams, people are quick to say they do. By digging a little deeper, you discover they're concocting their dreams on the spot. When asked if they have a written dream list, the answer is almost always no. The fact is that the majority of people are not dedicated to making their dreams come true and many don't dream at all.

Within a dream is the seed of a new reality.

To make your dreams come true, they must be specific and backed by absolute commitment.

The dreamers are the ones who achieve great things. All of us have the opportunity to guide our lives in any direction we choose. What you think and believe you can do, you will do. You can become or do almost anything you desire. In the word *desire* we find one of the secrets to success. When speaking of desire, I'm talking about a passion—an obsession. To hope for your dreams to come true is of no value.

This is the point where we separate the serious reader from the casual browser.

Please get a notebook and pen and allow forty-five minutes of quiet in a comfortable environment.

Write *My Dreams* at the top of the sheet and begin listing them. Don't limit yourself. At this point, it makes no difference whether you believe you can accomplish what you write down. Your dreams can range from having a million dollars in the bank to taking a trip to outer space. Once you begin the process, you'll find your imagination kicking in and the dreams will flow. You'll envision going on your own

When you read a necessary step to accomplish a goal, it's critical that you follow the instructions precisely.

If you have it in writing, you have a prayer; if you don't have it in writing, you have nothing but air.

African safari, having a personal tour of the Vatican, taking a hot air balloon ride over the Grand Canyon, finding your perfect mate, owning a 500-acre ranch, having an oceanfront home, driving a racecar, playing the violin at Carnegie Hall, retiring at fifty, designing and building your perfect home, playing golf at Pebble Beach and St. Andrews, having box seats at the Super Bowl

Please do not go any further until you complete this step.

or World Series, owning the racehorse that wins the Kentucky Derby. This is a list you'll need to save, refer to, and add to and subtract from as your dreams change. Your only limitations will be those you place on yourself.

As we delve further into the *How* of making your dreams come true, I'll give you everything you need, including a plan.

Thoughts become reality!

You will become what you think about. It all begins with a state of mind. No dream has ever come true that didn't begin as a thought. Every material thing you come into contact with was a thought before it became a reality. Even though you may have graduated from college, I'm betting you have not been trained in the importance of

The most important message in life is to learn what to think and then do it.

controlling your thoughts. Once you can read and write, your thoughts become the most important factor to your future. Since the late 1800s, great men and women have espoused teaching children the importance of their thoughts. It's

Your thoughts are a preview of your life's coming attractions.

hard to believe that we are in the twenty-first century and are still not doing it.

What we think about will determine the quality of our lives.

I'll explain the importance of your thought world shortly and how it ties into every aspect of your life.

Few people have been schooled in how to think or the magnitude of their thoughts. How you think is as much a habit as the time you go to bed or the number of cups of coffee you drink each morning. Effective thinking is necessary to make your dreams come true. You're who you are today because of your past thoughts. What is commonly known as character is actually the sum of your thoughts. If you're good or evil, kind or mean, optimistic or pessimistic, easy-going or stern, happy or sad, it's because of your thinking. This is a powerful truth because it means you're the creator of your destiny and the maker of your fate.

Your success or failure will be determined by your thinking.

Most people have wrestled with the question: is our life pre-destined or is it one of free will? You'll likely find the answer surprising, because it's both. It comes down to cause and effect.

Once you make your choice, the consequences are inescapable. Our existence is a series of effects that begin in thought. If we think good thoughts and do good deeds, we'll reap good consequences. By the same token, if we think evil thoughts and do evil deeds, we must suffer the sad consequences.

You have complete freedom to choose (free will) what to think or do, so you are without a doubt the cause. Once you make a choice, you must live with the effects, which are the consequences of your choice.

Once you know this truth, you'll want to rid yourself of all hateful, arrogant, unhealthy, evil, and selfish thoughts. From this point forward, you'll want to close your mind to all cynical and discouraging influences. Being susceptible to benighted influences is a pathway to disaster. Affirmative and negative thoughts or emotions cannot occupy your mind simultaneously. You and you alone control your thinking. Begin filling your mind with thoughts of satisfaction, prosperity, generosity, kindness, love, patience, forgiveness, and selflessness.

Your destiny is determined by your thoughts and actions.

Your ability to make your dreams come true depends on how you choose to think. Thoughts backed by desire will translate into their physical equivalents.

Please consider the previous sentence carefully, because with right thinking you'll take the first step toward making your dreams come true.

We don't see the world as it is—we see it as we are. You have literally thought yourself into the person you are today. You have also thought yourself into your current circumstances. Many say they're victims of circumstances, but that cannot be true. Two people often find themselves in the same situation yet have different outcomes. For example, imagine

Your outer world reflects your inner thoughts.

there's a fire in a neighborhood and two houses with all their contents burn to the ground. In both instances, the men lose their wives in the fire. One of the men becomes depressed and never recovers, living out his life in pain and sorrow. The other man says to himself: *I can't do anything about what's happened. I can rebuild my house and get new belongings and, in time, I can find another woman to love. I can still be a productive member of society. With proper thinking and hard work, I can once again have a satisfying life.* He goes on to lead a wonderful and successful life. The same circumstance happened to both, but the results were as different as night and day:

> *Circumstances can only affect you to the degree you let them.*

> *Thoughts only have the power you give them.*

> **Their fates were determined not by their circumstance but by their thinking.**

We can't always control our circumstances, but we can control our thoughts.

When you mix good thinking (generous and optimistic thoughts) with a definite purpose, you're on your way to making your dreams come true. The mind that doubts or fears repels prosperity. Remember—no one can do your thinking for you.

Control of your thoughts requires self-discipline; either you control your thoughts or they will control you. As you begin to think unselfish thoughts, the blessings you desire will come your way. As you improve your thought world, you will attract others who also dwell on this higher plane of consciousness. Soon, you'll find you're surrounded by those who share your values and virtues.

You are the only one who can alter your current condition and secure your future.

Your probability for success improves as your dreams become more specific and your thoughts become more vivid. Definiteness of purpose is an essential factor in making dreams come true. Definiteness of purpose means a crystal-clear objective and demands commitment and determination. Most failures are a result of hoping and wishing instead of committing and acting. A hope or wish is nothing more than a desire with no effort to make it happen.

To make your dreams come true, you must desire them with all your heart and soul.

This brings us to the importance of focus. To be successful requires concentrated thought. Your ability to make a dream come true multiplies tremendously when your physical and mental resources are focused.

When you're willing to stake your entire future on something, you will get it.

In today's world of multitasking, the majority of people have lost their focus. Few even have a single aim. Because of scattered energy, people experience anxiety and dissatisfaction and don't achieve their goals. You can't make dreams come true in bunches. You can make bunches of dreams come true but only one at a time.

Single-mindedness is power.

There's a good reason you're not at your best when you're on your computer and talking on the phone at the same time. You're not fully present for either. Focus on one task with commitment and watch your world improve.

Excellence, thoroughness, and success come from concentration.

To make a dream come true, you must clearly define what you want. It's not enough to say you want a car. You need to be very specific. What kind of car? What model? What color? Exactly what accessories? The more detailed you are, the more you enhance your chances of success.

Imagination plays a central role in success. The more vividly you imagine having what you want, the better your chances are of getting it. Your best bet is to get an actual picture of what you desire. Then look at that picture and imagine yourself in the driver's seat with your favorite CD playing while luxuriating in the smell of the leather interior. Feel the way it corners and experience in your mind its powerful acceleration.

There a reason for this process:

> ***When you continuously imagine thoughts, they become reality.***

It's important that you comprehend that last statement because it's one of the most important statements you'll ever read. Just reading something doesn't make it materialize. Reading with feeling and imagination will speed you toward your dream. To make your dreams come true, visualize what you want, see and feel yourself already in possession of it, then you'll start to comprehend that you can think your way to whatever you want.

QUIZ	**DO YOU THINK YOU HAVE WHAT IT TAKES TO MAKE YOUR DREAMS COME TRUE?**

1 You are sitting in front of the computer daydreaming about something wonderful happening to you. You ...

a Keep on daydreaming because it sure is fun to think about.

b Say to yourself, "Hey, that could happen to me."

c Think, "This is definitely going to happen to me one day, I know it."

2 You try out for something you really love, like the school play or a sports team, and you don't make it. You . . .

a Act like you didn't really want it anyway and look for something else to do in your spare time.

b Feel bad for a while but tell yourself stuff happens, maybe you'll try again next time.

c Decide to start practicing even harder so you can get better and try out again as soon as possible.

3 You tell somebody that you really like him/her, but the person says he/she just wants to be friends. You . . .

a Want to hide because you feel so embarrassed.

b Hope your friends don't find out, and if one of them mentions it, act like it didn't really matter.

c Tell your friends because even though you're embarrassed they can probably make you feel better.

QUIZ

DO YOU THINK YOU HAVE WHAT IT TAKES TO MAKE YOUR DREAMS COME TRUE? *(continued)*

4 When you hear stories about people who came to this country with nothing and then became rich and famous and did amazing things, you think . . .

a "Sure, they did it, but I'm not them."

b "I don't know that I could ever work that hard."

c "Hey, if they can do it, so can I."

5 When you find yourself dreaming about the great things you want to do in your life, you . . .

a Let yourself go, imagining all the details of how you'll make it happen and enjoy it.

b Fall asleep—might as well, it's only a dream anyway, right?

c Feel embarrassed and try to snap out of it. Why daydream when you could be doing something to make those great things happen?

6 If you ever told your friends about some of your big dreams, they would . . .

a Roll their eyes.

b Make fun, but then admit it's cool and maybe even say go for it.

c Tell you about their big dreams, too.

7) You hear that one of your friends writes down his dreams on a piece of paper and keeps it in his drawer. You think . . .

a It's kind of a geeky thing to do.

b If you're really determined, what difference does writing it down make?

c Hey, whatever works for him.

SCORE Count up the number of times you answered a, b, and c, then flip to the end of the chapter to find out what your score means.

BELIEF AND FAILURE

Failure is only a state of mind. You cannot fail until you accept defeat as reality. Failure is the inability to accomplish your goals. As long as you're working toward your objective, you haven't and cannot fail. Failure can't cope with persistence. Everyone who succeeds goes through periods of heartbreak and struggle. When discouragement sets in and the future looks bleak, remember that it's not that you've failed, it's only that you haven't succeeded yet. Each setback brings you closer to success. When one door closes, another one opens. Every *no* brings you closer to a *yes*. Failure comes in *cant's*, as in *I can't do this* and success comes in *cans,* as in *I can* and *I will.* Failure is a prerequisite to success. A boxer must learn to take punches to become a champion—each of us must learn to take the blows of life to achieve success. The mission is to keep moving toward your dream. Failure won't overtake you if your desire to succeed is sufficiently strong.

Please remove the words failure *and* can't *from your vocabulary.*

Belief is vital to making your dreams come true. There are few things that a strong belief and a burning desire cannot make possible. When you believe, you're giving power and life to your thoughts, which increases the odds of their physical manifestation. As discussed in chapter 2 on habits, the best way to get what you want is to get it into your subconscious. The only known way to accomplish that is by the repetition of affirmations.

You eventually come to believe whatever you keep telling yourself.

You have control of what reaches your subconscious; however, most people fail to use this power to positive effect. It's a power you may begin taking advantage of right this minute. Because of the significance of the subconscious, the following statement deserves your attention:

Never think or say anything about yourself that you don't want to be true.

How often do we hear statements like *I'm not good at directions . . . or spelling . . . or math . . . or remembering names . . . or being on time?* Every time you say or think negative things about your-self, you're reinforcing something you don't want to be true and get-ting your subconscious mind to accept it. The subconscious mind

> **The mind will eventually take on the nature of its dominating influences.**

does not differentiate between good and bad. From this point forward, only say or think the things about yourself that you want to be true. The more often you say and think them, the sooner they'll become reality. Begin now to think and say: *I'm a good student, a quick learner, a valuable employee, a good parent. I'm respon-sive, on time, resourceful, competent, thoughtful, kind, honest, generous, loving, and patient.* The more you tell yourself something, the sooner you become it.

QUIZ	CAN YOU DEAL WITH THE REALLY HARD STUFF?

1 I can't stand change—I would be happy staying in the same neighborhood and I even like eating the same foods all the time.

☐ Strongly Agree   ☐ Agree   ☐ Disagree   ☐ Strongly Disagree

2 When my friends get into big trouble, I panic and worry that something bad like that might happen to me.

☐ Strongly Agree   ☐ Agree   ☐ Disagree   ☐ Strongly Disagree

3 I like having a clear plan for how things should go, and when things don't go that way, it makes me really nervous.

☐ Strongly Agree   ☐ Agree   ☐ Disagree   ☐ Strongly Disagree

4 If somebody says something mean to me or hurts me, I remember every word and play it over and over in my head.

☐ Strongly Agree   ☐ Agree   ☐ Disagree   ☐ Strongly Disagree

5 Sometimes I feel really clueless about other people—I hear what they're saying but I find out later I totally missed what they really meant.

☐ Strongly Agree   ☐ Agree   ☐ Disagree   ☐ Strongly Disagree

6 I know other people say you should learn from your mistakes but how? I feel like I keep making the same mistakes over and over again.

☐ Strongly Agree   ☐ Agree   ☐ Disagree   ☐ Strongly Disagree

7 When I fail at something, I feel so humiliated I could almost throw up and I just want to hide out in my room for a long, long time.

☐ Strongly Agree   ☐ Agree   ☐ Disagree   ☐ Strongly Disagree

8 When I meet new people, I am more worried about what they will think of me and whether they will like me than whether I like them or would want to hang out with them.

☐ Strongly Agree   ☐ Agree   ☐ Disagree   ☐ Strongly Disagree

9 When I work with other people on a team, I am usually the realistic person who points out why a plan won't work, so we won't make mistakes and head off in the wrong direction.

☐ Strongly Agree   ☐ Agree   ☐ Disagree   ☐ Strongly Disagree

10 When I mess up, there's a little voice in my head that says, "What's wrong with you? Why do you always mess up?" I need that voice to keep me in line so I won't screw up next time.

☐ Strongly Agree   ☐ Agree   ☐ Disagree   ☐ Strongly Disagree

SCORE Give yourself 1 point for every "Strongly Disagree," 2 points for every "Disagree," 3 points for every "Agree," and 4 points for every "Strongly Agree." Then flip to the end of the chapter to find out what your score means.

ASSOCIATES/MENTORS

A key to success in any venture is the people with whom you choose to associate. You'll be raised up or pulled down to their level. We eventually emulate those we associate with most closely. There's a sound reason successful people associate with other successful people and failures hang out with failures. Birds of a feather *do* flock together. If you use what you learned in the human relations chapter, you know how to win with people who are more successful than you by offering them what they want. They are the faction who can help you make your dreams come true. Search out people you respect and admire, who have accomplished what you want to accomplish, and ask for their suggestions. *Then follow their advice.* One of the best ways to learn and accomplish things is following the advice of someone who has already achieved what you want. You may not have all the knowledge that you need, so you've got to know where and how to get it. Successful people have learned to rely on others in the areas where they're not competent. You'll need to associate with people who encourage you, want you to succeed, and help you to think and act for yourself. I attribute a great deal of my success to two such people. Because I listened and acted on what they said, they stuck with me and guided me through waters I could never have navigated alone. My problems seemed simple to them because of their experience and each suggestion they presented worked. Don't leave your associations to chance. Think about the qualities you admire and respect and find people to associate with who exhibit those qualities. Associating with the right people is a critical step toward your success.

Here are the specific steps to make your dreams come true.

I can't stress this enough:

If you want to make your dreams come true, you must commit to and act on exactly what is written next.

Your success will depend on your willingness to follow these instructions. The following steps *must be in writing.*

❶ Determine *exactly* what your dream is. It must be specific and detailed, such as "My dream is to acquire $1,000,000," rather than simply, "I want to make a lot of money." Or perhaps your dream is "I want to acquire a single-story, 2,500-square-foot home less than a mile from the sea, with a pool and tennis court. It must have at least one acre of property and be close to town." That's much more concrete than "I want a new house."

❷ Write down what you're willing to give in return for your dream. This may include working a second job, going to night school to increase your specialized knowledge, or learning a new profession. Perhaps you commit to putting into practice each of the principles discussed in chapter 1 or each of the habits discussed in chapter 2. *There's no such thing as something for nothing.* Sacrifices will be necessary to make your dreams come true.

❸ Name the precise date you expect your dream to come true.

❹ Write a plan to accomplish your dream. Be as detailed and specific as possible. As soon as you complete your plan, start following it.

❺ Write your dream on a 3×5 card; include the date you intend to achieve it, what you will give

to make it happen, and a brief description of
your plan.

6 Read what's written on your 3×5 card *out loud*
three times daily *until your dream comes true.*
Once in the morning when you get up, again
after lunch, and finally just before you go to bed.
Add emotion as you read, seeing and feeling as if
you have already accomplished your dream and
how wonderful it feels. *(This is a critical step and
must be done daily.)*

QUIZ   **ARE YOU A GOOD LISTENER?**

Who cares? Isn't being a good talker what really
counts? Not so much. Turns out people who have
good listening skills are considered more friendly,
competent, and smarter than people who don't.
Who wouldn't want that? Find out how you rate.

1 If someone is taking a long time to tell a story,
I'll finish his sentences just to help speed things
along.

a Most of the time
b Sometimes
c Not too often
d Hardly ever

QUIZ — **ARE YOU A GOOD LISTENER?** *(continued)*

2 When others talk I pay attention but I am also thinking about what I will say in response so the conversation won't have awkward pauses.

- **a** Most of the time
- **b** Sometimes
- **c** Not too often
- **d** Hardly ever

3 When someone tells me about a problem she's having, I tell her what I would do and I try to be helpful and point out where I think she messed up.

- **a** Most of the time
- **b** Sometimes
- **c** Not too often
- **d** Hardly ever

4 I try to repeat some of what someone has just said to me to let him know I understand what he's talking about.

- **a** Most of the time
- **b** Sometimes
- **c** Not too often
- **d** Hardly ever

5 I don't look other people in the eye for long when they're talking because I worry that it will make them uncomfortable or think I'm weird.

- **a** Most of the time
- **b** Sometimes
- **c** Not too often
- **d** Hardly ever

6 When I meet someone new, I am not comfortable asking her questions and so I'll mostly talk about myself.

- **a** Most of the time
- **b** Sometimes
- **c** Not too often
- **d** Hardly ever

7 I watch other people's facial expressions and body language while they're talking, so I can really understand what they mean.

- **a** Most of the time
- **b** Sometimes
- **c** Not too often
- **d** Hardly ever

8 I try to stay as still and quiet as I can while other people are talking—I don't want to nod

| QUIZ | **ARE YOU A GOOD LISTENER?** *(continued)* |

my head in agreement or smile or anything because it might distract them.

a Most of the time
b Sometimes
c Not too often
d Hardly ever

9 I feel weird asking people questions about their personal lives because I'm worried they'll think I'm just nosy.

a Most of the time
b Sometimes
c Not too often
d Hardly ever

10 I lose track of what other people are saying and find myself fidgeting or playing with anything that's nearby, like tapping a pencil or doodling.

a Most of the time
b Sometimes
c Not too often
d Hardly ever

SCORE	Count up your points, then flip to the end of the chapter to find out what your score means.

1	a. 1; b. 2; c. 3; d. 4	**6**	a. 1; b. 2; c. 3; d. 4
2	a. 1; b. 2; c. 3; d. 4	**7**	a. 4; b. 3; c. 2; d. 1
3	a. 1; b. 2; c. 3; d. 4	**8**	a. 1; b. 2; c. 3; d. 4
4	a. 4; b. 3; c. 2; d. 1	**9**	a. 1; b. 2; c. 3; d. 4
5	a. 1; b. 2; c. 3; d. 4	**10**	a. 1; b. 2; c. 3; d. 4

CONCLUSION

If understood and applied, what you've just read will make your dreams come true. The principles discussed here were responsible for my success and that of thousands of others. I began using these principles in the sixties while I was still a milkman. My first dream (one that seemed bigger than life to me) was to acquire $50,000. That was almost more money than I could imagine at the time. I wanted to put the formula I had learned to the test and prove to myself whether it worked. By following exactly what I have described to you, I accomplished that first dream in less than three years. I went on to dream more and, by following the same plan, was able to rise to the top of a Fortune 500 company, buy a new Mercedes, build a flourishing commercial real estate company, help improve hundreds of lives, marry my life's companion, and fly first class to Tahiti, Acapulco, London, South Africa, China, Hong Kong, Paris, Ireland, Scotland, New Zealand, Botswana, and Alaska. I was also able to build my dream house, become a racecar driver, own a champion racehorse, join the country clubs of my choice, play golf at Augusta National, Pebble Beach, and St. Andrews, achieve complete financial security, and retire at the age of fifty-five in Hawaii on a thirty-five-acre coffee farm.

I don't tell you this to boast but to inspire you and show you what you can achieve if you implement what you've read. You will fail if you pick and choose which parts of the instructions to follow.

If you follow the instructions exactly, you'll have the potential to achieve things beyond your wildest dreams. All of this must be done without violating the rights of others. Remember that temporary defeat is not failure. You'll have setbacks as do all who succeed. They are only tests of your persistence. There's no speculation in what has been written in this chapter. What you have read is a guaranteed formula for making your dreams come true. There's only one question:

Are you willing to supply the desire, definiteness of purpose, faith, patience, and persistence to follow the instructions exactly?

QUIZ **ANSWERS**

● **DO YOU THINK YOU HAVE WHAT IT TAKES TO MAKE YOUR DREAMS COME TRUE?**

What your score means:

MOSTLY As: You pride yourself on being realistic. That's a useful trait in life, but you also need to be a little less hard on yourself. Let yourself dream a little. The first step to making dreams come true is letting yourself have a dream to start with.

MOSTLY Bs: You've got a good balance between having realistic impulses and allowing yourself to have big dreams. You have to have both skills to make dreams come true—so keep working and keep dreaming.

MOSTLY Cs: You are open to big dreams—and you surround yourself with other people who have big dreams, too. Those are two important parts of making your dreams a reality one day. So keep on thinking big, sticking with friends who share your big dreams and encourage others to make their dreams come true, too. Hey, maybe they'll invite you on their yacht.

● CAN YOU DEAL WITH THE REALLY HARD STUFF?

What your score means:

If you scored between 30 and 40 points, you tend to be a little hard on yourself. Cut yourself some slack—everybody messes up. And everybody is embarrassed when they do. Remind yourself that it's not a big deal, just part of life, and you can get past it to better times.

If you scored between 10 and 29 points, you are the bounce-back wizard. You are able to come back after something bad happens and try again. Keep it up. And encourage your friends to do the same.

● ARE YOU A GOOD LISTENER?

What your score means:

If you scored between 10 and 29 points, listen up! The lower your score the more you need to practice listening—really paying attention and letting people know you understand what they say without judging, and without feeling you have to put in your two cents all the time.

If you scored between 30 and 40 points, you're a pretty good listener—you let others speak and you really listen. Keep it up, as it will pay off in work and in love.

DATING, MARRIAGE, AND PARENTING

My objective in this chapter is to give you information that will permit you to make good decisions about dating, marriage, and parenting. I'll begin with a personal story that is pertinent.

The following events took place in Fresno, California. I was only two years out of high school, living and working on a dairy farm. I occasionally frequented a café adjacent to the dairy. On one of those visits, a pretty young waitress named Patricia caught my eye and I asked her out. I learned she lived with her parents and had a three-year-old son named Ronnie. Even though we were only nineteen, we were married in less than a year. Before getting married, I'd discussed our plans with my dad; he advised me that I was much too young and should wait a few years. He knew what he was talking about, but I didn't listen. Now I want you to benefit from my experience. People who marry too young frequently miss out on the formative years of self-discovery and the formation of an independent identity, which will make them better marriage partners. Solicit, listen to, and weigh your parents' advice carefully because they have your best interests at heart and can help you avoid costly mistakes.

Patricia's parents had played a major role in raising Ronnie and were attached to him. When we told them our wedding plans, they insisted that Ronnie had to stay with them. Patricia was having no part of that. We tried reasoning and then pleading, all to no avail. They were determined to raise Ronnie, even though he was Patricia's son, so our only alternative was to slip away with Ronnie. Patricia carefully packed their belongings into a trunk and I parked in the driveway near the front door. The arrangement was to load the trunk and linger, waiting for just the right moment to make our getaway. Patricia's parents were wary and kept a close eye on Ronnie. I loaded the trunk and waited with the car running. I heard the screen door slam and looked up just in time to see Patricia running down the wooden stairs with Ronnie in tow. As soon as she was in the car, I heard another slam and glanced up to observe her dad sprinting toward us. I put the car in reverse and sped backward toward the main road. Patricia's dad almost reached us before we drove away and I still don't know how we escaped. I don't think my heart rate has been that high since that day. The only things missing were a shotgun and the dogs.

During our seven years of marriage, we had a daughter, Shirley, and a son, Jimmy. Patricia was a loving wife and mother. I was ambitious and had started my climb up the corporate ladder. The more wealth and authority I experienced, the more I wanted. We lived in Bakersfield; however, my sales territory was the Mojave Desert, selling to Edwards Air Force Base and China Lake Naval Base. I traveled a great deal and had embraced the fast life, compromising a lot of my values. After one of those trips, I came home and informed Patricia that I was leaving. That's a moment in time I'd like to take back, but there's nothing I can do about it now. As I drove away, I saw an innocent, caring wife and mother standing on the curb in front of our home, holding our baby boy. Ronnie was holding his mother's hand and Shirley was holding his. All four of them had tears streaming down their faces as I departed, chasing my selfish ambitions.

That occurrence is the most painful regret of my life. I'm ashamed to tell you this history, but I do so trusting it will help you avoid such deeds. There are several things you can realize from my mistakes:

1. Take time before getting married and consider all its long-term ramifications.
2. Have at least a year-long engagement.
3. Listen to wise, experienced counsel (like my dad's advice to wait).
4. Be sure you're marrying for the right reasons and not only because of the physical excitement you feel when dating.
5. Marriage is about trust and companionship, so be sure the person you marry can be your best friend.
6. Take your time before having children. They will be the greatest responsibility of your life. Children are precious and helpless and have little chance of success and happiness without the love and guidance of their parents.

Avoid making the same mistakes I did by considering the pain they can cause:

1. Not being with your children daily to help them grow up.

② Having to share the raising of your children.

③ Feeling you let them down.

④ Missing their special days.

⑤ Wondering for a lifetime about the closeness you could have had if you had been with them every day.

⑥ Watching everyone suffer trying to get comfortable after divorce.

⑦ Knowing you have taken away the safety net they so desperately needed.

The next few years were spent sowing the wild oats that I should have sown before marriage. One night at a Xerox party, I met an appealing, petite, brown-eyed girl with dark hair. We were getting to know each other when the host asked if I'd pick up some supplies for the party. I asked the young lady to accompany me; when we got to the street, there was a line of cars on both sides. I jokingly asked which car she'd like to take. Without hesitation, she pointed to a green Porsche Targa. I walked over, unlocked the door, and we drove off. I was delighted she'd selected my car. We began dating and I learned she'd worked for Xerox in New York, had been married twice, and had an eight-year-old daughter. She was smart, pretty, and unusually charming. About six months later, we decided to get married. One June day, we drove down to Pebble Beach and took our blanket out to the seventh tee and exchanged our vows.

Even though our relationship lasted many years, I didn't go into it for the right reasons. I wanted her because she was good-looking, smart, ambitious, and sophisticated. There's nothing wrong with any of those qualities—in fact, they are wonderful assets for anyone.

What you don't know can *hurt you and* *ignorance is* not *bliss.*

However, more than that is necessary to ensure an enduring marriage. I also needed to be sure she was the woman who would be my best friend, someone who demonstrated the virtues of humility, thoughtfulness, patience, compassion, tolerance, and generosity. I'm not suggesting she didn't have some of those virtues; it was more that I wasn't looking for them. I feel responsible for the eventual failure of the relationship—I believe if I'd had those virtues, she'd have been willing to do her part. Once again, I found myself in an awful situation, hurting not only my wife of sixteen years but also our sweet, innocent daughter. Life is a learning experience and the purpose of this book is to keep you from learning life's most important lessons the hard way.

I eventually got it right and married Lisa Michelle Ross, a young woman beautiful in body, heart, mind, and spirit, who I'd known for five years. We'd been friends and business associates all that time. The first time I met Lisa was when she came into the company for an interview to head up our administration department. One of the things I'll never forget is that she sat down and looked me right in the eye. I don't think she took her eyes off mine for the full hour that I spoke with her. I had never seen anyone with that quality of eye contact. After the interview, I suggested that she would be a natural in sales and offered her a job as my assistant once she got the administration department organized. Six months later, we began working together and her career soared. She was the best I'd ever seen at customer relations and initiating new business. She was a dedicated worker, starting at 6:00 in the morning and often still working at 6:00 at night. We turned out to be a good team and never spoke a cross word. We were both married and the thought that we would ever have a non-business relationship never crossed either of our minds. As the years went by, my marriage began heading in the wrong direction. Little did I know at the time that Lisa's was suffering the same fate. Neither of our marriages lasted and we began a relationship that has been almost perfect ever since. As long as I've known Lisa, she's been one of the most thoughtful, kind, loving, family oriented, smart, and witty people I've ever met. She's loved by everyone who knows her. We've been married sixteen years and each of them has been memorable. She's helped me realize the importance of family. She's my best friend; since I've retired, we've been together almost every day. Lisa hails from Columbus, Ohio, and is a dedicated Buckeye.

My goal is to provide you information that will help you find the right spouse the first time around and have the rest of your life to enjoy the union.

DATING

Dating should be a gratifying and learning experience. I'll cover what I've learned with you so your dating experience can be a beneficial one. Dating is your chance to discover what's important to you in a relationship. It requires some experience to uncover the qualities you'll want in a spouse. Dating will be more enjoyable if you approach it as an adventure by not taking it too seriously in the beginning. Think of it as a treasure hunt.

Avoid the common mistake of basing your decision about who to date solely on looks. You shouldn't go out with anyone who's not appealing to you, but you can miss the good ones if you focus too much on appearance. The athlete or model may look great, but is frequently preoccupied with his or her physical appearance and may not have the enduring virtues you seek. People who are self-absorbed won't have emotional room for you. Exceptionally good-looking people are exciting at first but won't withstand the test of time unless there's also beauty on the inside. Ask yourself a few probing questions about the kind of people you want to date:

> *Do they share your values? Are they thoughtful, considerate, giving, happy, and fun?*

If you can answer *yes* to those questions, you're on the right track. If you find your date is selfish, rude, pessimistic, arrogant, lazy, or mean, think vigilantly before going any further. Any one of those qualities signals danger. Create a list of virtues that are important to you and it will help you narrow the field.

I'll discuss some of the physical aspects of dating first because this is so important to both men and women. Men, in particular, can be overly focused on the purely physical. This is a part of men's nature and it's important for both sexes to understand it. Women have an equally strong sex drive, but it is, as a rule, more discriminating. How you choose to deal with the physical aspects of dating is personal and I make no judgment about what's right or wrong. I have suggestions, but you're the only one who will know what's right for you.

Always be true to your self. Don't be pushed, bullied, or coerced into doing anything you don't want to do.

You may choose to marry before having sex and that's admirable. You'll be proud and feel strong about yourself if you make that decision. It's a road rarely traveled but one with many benefits. If you choose to be intimate when dating, take it slow. There are many rewards to a slower, more romantic courtship.

The wise person will start the dating process by taking time to get to know the other person. Enjoy the process and be slow about even holding hands. Make the first kiss memorable. Make your kisses something to anticipate and not be taken for granted. Don't go past the kissing stage until trust is established. Keep the pace slow and honest for both your sakes. Those who heed this recommendation will hold on to the person they desire more often than those who don't and if the relationship doesn't last you'll have no regrets. It's human nature to take for granted the things you can have at will. If you make your date earn his or her way, you'll feel good about yourself and your date will be proud to be with you.

THE BOY/GIRL THEORY

You'll want to employ the boy/girl theory for maximum enjoyment when dating. This theory is equally valuable in business, parenting, and friendship. The boy/ girl theory involves practicing patience and resisting instant gratification. Seeking instant gratification can lead to short-term pleasure but frequently causes long-term pain. An example of this is being out on a date and letting yourself go too far in order to satisfy your immediate craving, later to realize you did so with the wrong person, causing you to have long-term regrets. It's worse yet to go too far without taking the time to use protection and becoming pregnant or being responsible for the cost and responsibilities of raising a child. Similar problems arise from instant gratification when it comes to eating, spending, and other forms of pleasure-seeking. Remind yourself that nature never acts in haste and, because you're part of nature, neither should you. People covet what's hard to get and regularly take for granted what they can have at will. The more someone pushes, the more you resist. The more you're denied what you want, the more you want it. Let's say you've applied for a job and after the interview you call daily for a status report. After a few days, they stop taking your calls because you've become an irritation. Your odds of getting the job worsen with each call. Managers resist hiring people who appear desperate. People resist dating people who seem needy.

The most desirable people are captivating, command your respect, set boundaries, are considerate, retain their dignity, and have lives of their own.

The slightly elusive person is more desired than the one at your beck and call. Whether it's being asked out on a date, being kissed, or talking on the phone, it will serve you well not to be too eager, needy, or always available. The person who is not readily available is generally more intriguing. I'm not suggesting game-playing; I'm advising decoding human nature. Few of us want to be with the person who's there every time we turn around. Not many people want a person who shows up uninvited. It's hard to respect the person who allows you to call for a date at the last minute repeatedly and is still happy to go with you. I don't know anyone who respects those qualities.

You'll long for the person who keeps the relationship fresh, interesting, and exciting. Being a bit unpredictable and independent will make you more preferred. You're better off not being able to get everything you want exactly when you want it. Anticipation is a superb feeling. Be thoughtful and considerate, but don't always be accessible. To obtain the most gratifying and fulfilling relationship you can have, don't be a doormat, keep your relationships fresh and respectful, make sure to have a life of your own, and encourage your partner to do the same.

| QUIZ | IS THIS PERSON RIGHT FOR YOU? |

It isn't always easy to know whether the person you're with is the right one for you when you first start dating—or even later on. But here are some things to ask yourself to figure it out. Remember, there are no right or wrong answers—it's all about finding out how you feel.

1 The person I am seeing makes me feel confident and even sexy.

- **a** Yes, nearly all the time
- **b** Sometimes
- **c** No, hardly ever
- **d** Not sure

2 I like hanging out with this person, even when we're doing something I don't normally enjoy.

- **a** Yes, nearly all the time
- **b** Sometimes
- **c** No, hardly ever
- **d** Not sure

| QUIZ | **IS THIS PERSON RIGHT FOR YOU?** *(continued)* |

3 I like to try to think up things to do that will please my boyfriend/girlfriend—and he/she does the same for me.

- **a** Yes, nearly all the time
- **b** Sometimes
- **c** No, hardly ever
- **d** Not sure

4 I feel like he/she likes me just the way I am, flaws and all.

- **a** Yes, nearly all the time.
- **b** Sometimes
- **c** No, hardly ever.
- **d** Not sure

5 If I don't see this person for a few days, I really miss him/her.

- **a** Yes, nearly all the time
- **b** Sometimes
- **c** No, hardly ever
- **d** Not sure

SCORE Count up the number of times you answered a, b, c, and d, then flip to the end of the chapter to find out what your score means.

THE SELF SCALE

I developed the self scale as a consequence of many years spent studying relationships. Its purpose is to assist you in evaluating the risk involved in any new relationship. It will aid you to make the best decision possible regarding who to date, who to choose as a friend, who has the potential to be the best employer, and who to marry. When considering a new relationship, rate the person in question on the self scale. The selfless person displays love, humility, generosity, kindness, thoughtfulness, patience, forgiveness, compassion, approval, sympathy, and tolerance. Some may view these virtues as a form of weakness, but the opposite is true. These virtues represent an incredibly confident and genuine person. They keep the spotlight on others. They look out for others' best interests. The higher they rate, the less your risk and the lower they rate, the higher your danger. Each display of selfishness is a flashing red warning light.

If it's all about them, it's not going to be about you.

To enjoy a meaningful long-lasting relationship, you'll need to be with a giver, not a taker. Now, rate yourself on the self scale because you'll only attract a selfless person if you are one.

SELF SCALE QUESTIONNAIRE

By carefully rating yourself in each of the following
categories, you can determine your own self scale
rating or that of anyone with whom you're considering
having a relationship. It's advisable to review your own
answers with a trusted friend because we often don't see
ourselves as others see us. Rate each question on a scale
of 1–10 with 10 being the best and 1 being the worst.
On this questionnaire, the maximum possible score is
310 points and the minimum is 31. To assure you of
the best chance for a lasting, meaningful relationship, I
recommend a minimum score of 221 points.

1. Patient and kind when things don't go his or her way
2. Good listener
3. Asks lots of questions about others
4. Genuinely interested in others
5. Lets others go, be, and do things first
6. Calm, affirmative, and happy demeanor
7. Smiles a lot
8. Willing to try things others want to do
9. Thinks of others' comfort before his or her own
10. Remembers other people's special days like birthdays and anniversaries

11 Practices praise
12 Complimentary
13 Generous
14 Humble
15 Forgiving
16 Appreciative
17 Thoughtful
18 Honest
19 Good manners
20 Quick to help
21 Respectful
22 Willing to compromise
23 Loving
24 Punctual
25 Empathetic
26 Likes children
27 Appreciates nature
28 Exceeds your expectations
29 Good control of emotions
30 Kind
31 Embraces self-improvement

Identify the virtues that will improve your life the most and go to work on them.

CONCLUSION ON DATING

Enjoy your dating experiences until you're ready to get married. If you find your perfect soul-mate before you're ready for marriage, take pleasure in a long engagement and spend your time getting to know each other. The more you know about your potential spouse, the higher your odds are for a flourishing marriage. Ideally, the man will be five to ten years older because men mature slower than women. When you're young, your hormones are raging. It's important to base your decision about who to date seriously more on the person's virtues than on sex appeal. The physical becomes less important after a few years. How you are treated is always paramount.

Remember the self scale, evaluate your date based on his or her selflessness, and find yourself a person who rates high. Pay particular attention to that person's virtues, including: humility, kindness, thoughtfulness, self-discipline, compassion, generosity, self-responsibility, sense of humor, and wisdom. The more virtues the person has, the better your chances of a happy, long-term relationship.

QUIZ	**WILL THIS RELATIONSHIP LAST?**

Nobody has a crystal ball to see into the future. But some feelings are good signs that things will only get better—and others are red flags that a relationship is going nowhere. You can do a little fortune-telling for yourself by considering these questions:

1 My boyfriend/girlfriend tries really hard to get along with my friends and show me that he/she likes them (even when he/she doesn't like all of them).

☐ Yes   ☐ No

2 He/she often makes jokes at my expense and it really hurts my feelings.

☐ Yes   ☐ No

3 I feel like I have to make more sacrifices in this relationship than he/she does.

☐ Yes   ☐ No

4 When he/she messes up, he/she apologizes and acts like he/she's really sorry about it.

☐ Yes   ☐ No

| QUIZ | **WILL THIS RELATIONSHIP LAST?** *(continued)* |

5 I often feel that he/she pressures me to do what he/she wants and he/she doesn't really listen to what I want to do.

☐ Yes   ☐ No

6 When the two of us are alone, I feel relaxed and happy to be right where I am.

☐ Yes   ☐ No

7 I like it when we're alone together, but it's more fun when we're hanging out together in a group.

☐ Yes   ☐ No

8 He/she does some things I really don't like, but I am sure he/she will change if we get really serious.

☐ Yes   ☐ No

9 I am afraid to talk about some things that bother me in our relationship because I think he/she might break up with me.

☐ Yes   ☐ No

10 We like doing things together, but we also have things that we like doing separately.

☐ Yes   ☐ No

SCORE	Count up your points, then flip to the end of the chapter to find out what your score means.

1 T - 2 points; F - 1 point   **6** T - 2 points; F - 0 points

2 T - 0 points; F - 2 points   **7** T - 1 point; F - 2 points

3 T - 0 points; F - 2 points   **8** T - 0 points; F - 2 points

4 T - 2 points; F - 0 points   **9** T - 0 points; F - 2 points

5 T - 0 points; F - 2 points   **10** T - 2 points; F - 0 points

MARRIAGE

Who you marry is probably the most important decision of your life.

Getting out of a marriage is a lot harder than getting into one.

Take your time with this significant decision and enjoy the process. The right spouse will make life pleasant and meaningful in ways no one can experience alone.

1. The right person for you will be compatible with your core values. Take the time to make a list of them and see how a particular person measures up.

2. Ask yourself: *what makes this person the right one for me?* If you're marrying someone because of what he or she possesses or what you think he or she can do for you, you're barking up the wrong tree.

3. Marry someone because you respect and admire that person.

4. Marry someone because you make a good team and fill each other's emotional and physical needs.

5. The person you marry must be your best friend and the central person in your life.

6. Your perfect spouse will be similar to you in opinions and values. If you settle for someone who isn't, you will pay dearly later.

7. You can be sure you're moving in the right direction if you can say: *I like me best when I'm with you.*

If you think you're going to change the person you marry, you're sadly mistaken. You don't want anyone changing you and your spouse doesn't want you changing him or her either. When dating or engaged, you see the best someone has to offer. If you can't accept a person at that stage, you'll regret going forward. Everybody puts their best foot forward when dating. Keeping that in mind, if you find your prospective spouse is mean, angry, inconsiderate, lazy, stingy, possessive, arrogant, or selfish when dating or during your engagement, it will be best for you to reconsider. These traits go from bad to worse as people go from being on their best behavior to normal behavior. Be sure you're ready to accept your potential spouse as is before planning to wed. If the person doesn't change in the way you hope, will you be happy? If the answer is no, abort. Don't get so attached to the idea of marriage that you are willing to compromise on the core issues. Your true soul-mate is out there, so practice patience.

Marriages are lasting and satisfying when spouses love each other and put each other's needs and interests first. You'll want a spouse who cares about you and looks out for you. A good spouse will make you feel loved, valued, and understood. A good marriage is a partnership where the responsibilities are shared equally. If both work outside the home, both need to help with the grocery shopping and household chores. The last one to use the bed should make it. The cook shouldn't have to do the dishes. When you contribute equally, you have a chance for a magnificent marriage. Avoid any form of moodiness and be the bigger person when necessary. You'll enjoy doing nice things for each other.

One sure way to improve your probability for a good marriage is to gain an understanding of how your spouse wants to be treated. Many books have been written on the differences between men and women. Here, I'm interested in the similarities.

The only sensible approach is to spend time finding out how your spouse wants to be treated and then treat him or her that way.

What amazes me is the wonderful life that can be lived when you have the perspectives of both men and women. It seems true that neither sex is as effective alone as they are when working in concert with each other. I don't know how many times I have felt my wife did not understand something, only to find out she understood it better than I did.

Men and women differ in numerous ways and sometimes they make the mistake of treating the other the way they want to be treated.

We've been trained to do unto others as we would have them do unto us. The Golden Rule for dealing with people should be:

Treat other people the way they want to be treated.

Not only do men and women not want to be treated like the opposite sex, they often don't even want to be treated like people of their own sex. They simply want to be treated as individuals.

Here are some examples of not following this philosophy: a woman gives her husband an all-day pass for a local spa for Valentine's Day, not realizing he would not be caught dead in a spa. If he did not know her preferences, he might buy her a new vacuum cleaner for Christmas and she could be crushed that he didn't get her something more personal. She carefully wraps a gift for him and selects just the right card, not realizing he hardly notices the wrapping paper or the card but appreciates the gift. He gives her a nice gift with no card and she may feel slighted. She continually does the things for him that she wants done for her and vice versa. So here's the first rule for a better marriage:

> *Treat your spouse the way he or she wants to be treated, not the way you want to be treated.*

Now let's study some specifics.

LISTENING IS CRITICAL

Whether you're a man or woman, you want your spouse to listen when you're talking to him or her. Not being listened to is one of the primary complaints marriage counselors hear. It's important to learn how to listen to your spouse. The only way I know to do that is to ask questions about how your spouse wants you to listen. For example, it's not uncommon for spouses to want to talk about a problem they are dealing with just to get it off their mind and share it with their closest friend. Frequently, they may only want their mates to listen and be sympathetic; they may not be looking for them to solve the problem or tell them what they should do. Spouses who don't know this may jump in to try to resolve the matter. Astute spouses learn to listen and then inquire whether their loved ones are looking to solve the issue or just air it out. It's much better to ask whether an issue can be brought up later than to pretend to listen and not understand what is really being said. Be the one who cares enough to pay attention when your spouse is talking. Listen for the deeper meaning of the words. Make it easy to share things with you that are hard to talk about. When you are listening, you are paying your spouse the utmost respect. If you are not a good listener, please go back to chapter 1 and review listening skills. Being an effective listener is critical to a good marriage.

CONSISTENCY BUILDS TRUST

Consistency is a key to maintaining a loving relationship. Big mood swings are difficult to deal with. Be the spouse who is consistent all the time about helping with the chores, calling when running late, and remembering special dates. Be the one who shows appreciation for small acts of kindness. Avoid raising your voice or being mean in any way. Pick each other up when down and make it a habit to think of what is best for your mate. Be the person your spouse can count on in the areas that matter most. Consistency pays big dividends.

MAKE EACH OTHER FEEL SPECIAL

Be the man who selects where to take your wife, makes the reservations, and reserves that special table. Be the woman who surprises her husband with seats to see his favorite team play. Bring each other little surprises like a favorite ice cream or wine. Acknowledge and show appreciation when she makes a good meal. Tell him how much you appreciate it when he drives the five hours to one of your favorite getaways. Help with the dishes, open doors, and hold her coat. If you drive your spouse's car, have it washed and fill it up with gas. Cherish each other and practice being respectful. Anticipate each other's needs and let your spouse know often that you love him or her. Occasionally surprise each other with a cold bottle of fine champagne or some special music.

GOOD COMMUNICATION IS VITAL

It takes time and effort to learn to communicate effectively. One of you may talk more than the other, one may talk in more extreme terms, and one of you may go into great detail while the other only deals with the basic points. Be patient with each other and discuss your likes and dislikes about the way you communicate. If you don't like too many details, make that request; by the same token, if you want more details, ask for them. Good communication is a little like learning to ride a horse in that you have to get into the rhythm of the horse; by the same token, you need to get into the rhythm of the way your spouse likes to communicate.

In a good relationship, both spouses want to give the other what they want and directness is the best way to accomplish that and avoid conflict.

One of the reasons you may get frustrated and feel your spouse doesn't listen is because you lose his or her attention along the way. Your spouse starts out paying attention and caring about what you have to say, but as you keep talking, he or she begins to be unsure where the conversation is going and wonders if there's going to be a point to the story. The following example is humorous and a little extreme, but the humor comes from the fact there's a lot of truth to it. In this case, I'm telling the story with the woman being the speaker, but it's equally true when the man is the speaker.

If the dog had puppies today, the best approach is to say, "Victor, guess what? My dog had her puppies today." However, your boyfriend can get quite frustrated if you say, "Victor, I've got something exciting to tell you, but I also had the worst experience this morning. At eight o'clock, I was preparing toast and coffee and I burned the toast because my mother called and I lost all track of time. You know how my mom can carry on and the first thing I knew an hour had elapsed. I finally get off the phone and the doorbell was ringing. It was my sister wanting to know if I'd watch her baby. Her baby is so cute. She had her wrapped in a pink blanket with a little pink hat and these tiny pink shoes. I've been thinking perhaps one day we will have one. What do you think? I finally got dressed and just as I stepped outside it started pouring down rain. My hair got soaked and I looked like a drowning rat by the time I got to the store. You would not have believed the number of cars in the parking lot. It felt like it was the Fourth of July. Anyway, you know how much I love my dog, Lady. Well, she's pregnant and today she seemed very sick when I got back home so I decided to take her to the vet. You know— the one on Cypress Street next to the pizza place we like so much. We haven't been there in such a long time. Maybe we should plan to go this week. Would you enjoy that?" By this time, your boyfriend is lost, bored, not interested, and wondering if this story will ever end. For both your sakes, please just say:

The dog had puppies.

Being a good listener is necessary for good communication. With good communication, you can resolve most of your problems without conflict.

EXTREME WORDS ARE DANGEROUS

Some people use extreme words as a matter of course and most of us use them when trying to make an important point or win a disagreement. Extreme words can confuse your spouse and cause misunderstandings. Frequently, one of the two partners takes words literally; in that case, extreme words can cause heartache and confusion. Words like *always, never, everyone, no one, everything*, and *nothing* are rarely what we really mean. When one spouse says you *never* listen to me, it usually means you're not listening to me now. When your spouse says you *always* gawk at the opposite sex, he or she means *you just looked at someone in a way that upsets me*. Either party can take great exception to these extreme statements. Learn to say what you really mean by choosing the right words. Discuss extreme words when they bother you so both of you learn to avoid them.

DON'T EXPECT YOUR SPOUSE TO READ BETWEEN THE LINES

Communication problems arise when either party doesn't say what he or she means. Relying on innuendos and expecting your companion to interpret them is a formula for disaster. As a rule, men are not especially good at reading between the lines. The best bet for both sexes is to say specifically what you mean or want. If you want a hug or kiss, don't expect your spouse to read your mind or respond to your hints. Just tell or show your spouse what you want. If you're not sure you understand what your spouse means, ask for clarification, so you get the intended message. This is one of those places to keep it simple. Say what you mean and ask for what you want.

SUPPORT EACH OTHER

If your spouse is upset with anyone, be sure to take your spouse's side—it hurts if you side with the other person. Your partner may not always be right but always needs your support; feelings will be crushed if your partner doesn't get it. Even if you don't agree, let your spouse know you understand and sympathize and that you'd probably feel the same way if you were in similar circumstances. Assure your spouse you're both on the same team to stay.

TIMELINESS

There are exceptions, but spouses often show less respect for each other's time than they do with others. It's a bad habit not to be ready for your spouse at the appointed time. It shows carelessness and a lack of respect. The best plan is to be on time for everyone and at all times. Short of that ideal, it's most important to show that respect to your spouse.

Men want their wives to look good and that takes time. Women have to deal with many more contingencies than men when getting ready. Just fixing their hair may take forty-five minutes whereas men might only take five. Women deal daily with various forms of makeup and accessories. What to wear is more complicated for the woman. The man usually wears clothes he's worn many times before. Because you want your woman to look her best, it's imperative that you show patience and understanding with time in this area. A good rule of thumb is for the man to pad the real departure time by fifteen minutes and keep it to himself.

LAMENTING AND SPECULATING ARE TIME-WASTERS

In a marriage, there's no point in being mournful or whining about past events that can't be changed. Doing so serves no useful purpose and is exasperating. If someone hurt your feelings and you don't plan to do anything about it, move on. What good does it do to tell your spouse about it? If you were careless and put a dent in the car, move on. No amount of talking or lamenting will take the dent out. If something is in the past and cannot be corrected or if there's no meaningful lesson to be learned or remembered, forget it. Keep your thinking positive. Everyone you're around will feel better when you take that approach and you'll feel better about yourself.

What's the rationale behind trying to figure out why someone did or didn't do something? You sent a thoughtful gift to a friend and got no response, so you ask your spouse why he or she thinks your friend didn't respond. You might as well ask why water is wet. Your spouse has no more idea than you do. Speculation is guessing and guessing leads to trouble. It makes no sense to speculate about why people do things. The only rational action is to ask the person who did it why he or she did it. The same logic applies to questions like: *Do you think it's going to rain today? Should I take a sweater? Will olive oil work just as well as peanut oil? Do you think the Steelers will win today?* Learn to be self-reliant and make these decisions for yourself. Your spouse has no more insight than you about such questions and those kinds of questions may make him or her short-tempered with you.

LEARN EACH OTHER'S HOT BUTTONS

Instructing or criticizing a spouse is certain to create aggravation. Both of you are adults and have gotten to this point in life without someone looking over your shoulder. Comments like: *You're driving too fast . . . Don't you think that's enough salt in the mashed potatoes? . . . Don't drink out of the carton . . . Why don't you park over there? . . . Don't you think you've had enough to drink? . . . Take your feet off the coffee table . . . Why don't you order something different tonight? . . . Did you remember to take out the trash? . . . Haven't you watched enough sports for one day?* or *Do you have to call your mother* every *day?* all lead to trouble. Respect your spouse by not correcting him or her unless there is danger or you're looking for trouble. Let your spouse be if you want to be content together. I can assure you no one likes being told what to do. Pick your battles carefully and make sure it really matters before you ask your spouse to change his or her behavior. You will have a better relationship if you bite your tongue when tempted to instruct or criticize.

RECAPPING THE DAY

It's difficult enough getting through the workday without being asked to go over it when you get home. It isn't that your spouse doesn't want to talk to you; it's just that he or she usually doesn't want to relive the day. Your best option for good conversation is talking about subjects of mutual interest. The best plan is focusing on things unrelated to work. You'll have a finer relationship by discussing subjects you both enjoy.

ELIMINATE ALL CRITICISM

In a good relationship, the man and woman want to please each other above all else. When one makes the other feel like a failure, it hurts deeply and the hurt spouse may react poorly. Typical

Criticism is the surest and fastest way I know to ruin a relationship.

responses might be: *If you don't like the way I'm driving, keep it to yourself . . . If you're so smart, why don't you fix it? . . . Why bother to ask me? You seem to have all the answers . . . If I wanted to park over there, I would have.* Avoid offering unsolicited advice and any form of criticism. You may think you're being helpful, but to your spouse, it's disapproval. A spouse who wants your advice will ask for it. *Eliminate criticism and you'll prevent many arguments.* Any time you find yourself about to criticize, hold your breath and count to ten. The solution to eliminating criticism is learning to practice praise. Praise your spouse for what he or she is doing that you like and you'll see more of it. Please understand that criticism is ruinous and eliminate it.

WHEN TO LEAVE YOUR SPOUSE ALONE

We usually want to think our problems through before involving our spouse. It takes some time to get over it when something has upset us. Give your spouse some room and let him or her think it through and you'll get the best results. The worst thing you can do is follow your spouse around asking what's wrong. He or she will recover sooner if you'll let things be until your spouse comes back to you. It's best to let the person who has been upset dictate when and if to talk about the issue.

CONCLUSION ON MARRIAGE

What's the hardest year of marriage? Many would answer: *the one you're in.* I have good news for you. Each year of your marriage can be better than the last if both of you are determined for it to be that way. If only one of you is committed to making it better, it will get worse. A

Make praise and appreciation the cornerstone of your marriage.

successful marriage is built on good communication. Reread chapter 1 if you have any questions about how to improve your communication.

Keep telling your spouse what he or she is doing right. You'll soon be able to overlook the things you once found annoying.

Arguing is a cancer that will destroy a marriage. When Lisa and I got married, we had our share of arguments. Neither of us wanted arguing to be part of our lives, so we took a stand against it. We started by agreeing to go a month without an argument. We didn't succeed at first but kept trying and soon we made it through a month. It helped us to use a time-out when we sensed an argument starting. Things always looked better the next day when our emotions had calmed down. We set six months as our next target and made it. Now we have gone thirteen years without an argument, which proves it can be done. Our relationship improved immensely when the arguments stopped and we've had harmony in our home ever since. We certainly don't agree all the time, but we've learned we don't have to be attached to or defend our point of view. We chose not to argue and so can you.

Marriages follow the same pattern as moods— some days you're in a good mood and others you're not. Similarly, on some days your marriage seems perfect and on other days you wonder why on earth you got hitched. When your mood isn't good, you do the best you can, stay optimistic, count your blessings, and smile. Your marriage is no different. On the rough days, learn to remember the good ones, maintain a positive attitude, look for what's pleasing, stay away from blame, and give thanks for all the things you appreciate about your spouse. The trouble comes when you start to think *Oh, poor me.* Focus on all that's right instead of wallowing in what's wrong. No good ever comes from negative thinking.

When one spouse has a complaint, he or she should be able to say to the other *I would never treat you that way.*

Those are powerful words that go a long way toward solving problems. Be the one who can say *You know I wouldn't raise my voice to you. You know I'd protect you in this situation. You know I'd call and let you know if I were going to be that late.*

Are you aware that you have an emotional bank account with each person with whom you deal? With every interaction, you're either making deposits or withdrawals. The more you interact with anyone, the more deposits and withdrawals are made. It's especially important to understand this concept when dealing with your spouse, children, close friends, and employers. Every helpful act you do for anyone is a deposit and each harmful act is a withdrawal. Over time, your accounts grow or shrink depending on your actions. The higher your account, the more leniency you get; the smaller the account, the less the grace. For example, let's say you make a commitment to your wife that you'll develop the discipline of being prompt. Each time you live up to that commitment, you add to your emotional bank account with her. After weeks of not being late, you've built up a big account. For whatever reason, one day you slip. Your wife doesn't even mention it and gives you grace because you've been consistently on time. If you make the same agreement and are late often, your emotional bank account is overdrawn and criticisms and arguments will follow. One sure way to have success in marriage is to build up your emotional bank account in the areas of listening, loyalty, keeping your word, awareness, being on time, being generous, showing compassion and respect, and setting aside time for each other.

A marriage is like a piece of fine china. It has a beautiful ring, but once it has even a small crack, the ring is not the same.

1 Practice loving and kind speech. Harsh words can never be taken back.

2 Take it upon yourself to be the bigger person when necessary.

3 Build your marriage through praise, appreciation, and approval.

4 Learn to laugh together. Welcome humor. Create a light-hearted atmosphere.

5 Practice the things you want in your marriage and they will be there.

6 You'll be giving yourself a gift if you treat your spouse with respect and love.

7 Treat your spouse the way he or she wants to be treated.

8 Let love be the basis of all your words and actions.

QUIZ	**CAN YOU SPOT SIGNS OF LOVE-TROUBLE?**

There is nothing wrong with having disagreements—every relationship has moments you wish didn't happen. But some signs of trouble in relationships are more serious than others—and could be deal-breakers. Can you spot the warning signs that tell you it's time to move on and find somebody new?

1 He/she loves me so much that he/she's really jealous and doesn't want me talking to a potential partner.

☐ True   ☐ False

QUIZ	**CAN YOU SPOT SIGNS OF LOVE-TROUBLE?** *(continued)*

2 We don't have a lot in common—different religions, different backgrounds, and different ideas of what to do for fun—but that just adds to the excitement. After all, opposites attract.

☐ True   ☐ False

3 He/she has hit me, but he/she promised never to do it again.

☐ True   ☐ False

4 He/she drinks a lot now and does some other stuff that makes me uncomfortable, but I am sure that if we get married and have kids, he/she will finally grow up.

☐ True   ☐ False

5 I feel like he/she gets his/her way most of the time and I am the one who always has to give in.

☐ True   ☐ False

6 When we disagree about things, even small things, it often ends up in a fight or he/she just shuts me out completely.

☐ True   ☐ False

7 We don't have the same ideas about having children, but I am sure if he/she loves me enough I'll be able to talk him/her into my way of thinking.

☐ True   ☐ False

SCORE	Count up the your points, then flip to the end of the chapter to find out what your score means.

1 T - 5 points; F - 1 point   **5** T - 5 points; F - 1 point

2 T - 5 points; F - 1 point   **6** T - 5 points; F - 1 point

3 T - 10 points; F - 1 point   **7** T - 5 points; F - 1 point

4 T - 5 points; F - 1 point

PARENTING

Sometimes we learn valuable lessons from our children. A man punished his three-year-old daughter for wasting a roll of gold wrapping paper. Money was tight and he became upset because she used the entire roll trying to decorate a box to put under the Christmas tree. The little girl brought the gift to her father the next morning and said, "This is for you, Daddy." He was embarrassed by his earlier overreaction, but his anger flared again when he found that the box was empty. He said to her, "Don't you know when you give someone a present, there's supposed to be something inside?" The little girl looked up at him with tears in her eyes and said, "Daddy, it's not empty. I blew kisses into the box and they were all for you." The father was crushed. He put his arms around his little girl, and begged her forgiveness. He kept that gold box by his bed for years. Whenever he was discouraged, he'd take out an imaginary kiss and remember the love of the child who put it there.

When you become a parent, it's probably the greatest responsibility of your life. It's remarkable how little training we receive in such a vital area. My biggest regret is not being the father I could have been. You don't get a do-over on this responsibility and your children will be grown before you know it. My intention is to help you avoid the mistakes I made.

The first seven years are the most critical in the training of your child. These are the years in which your children will establish their habits and values. It's when they are especially malleable and it gives you an opening to teach them the behaviors they'll need for a successful life. As a young father, I was unaware of the sensitivity of a young child. I realize now that a raised voice is amplified many times in their tiny world. Only a soft voice filled with kindness and love is appropriate when speaking to them. Their parents are their world and they need to feel safe and loved. One of the greatest gifts a father can give his children is to love their mother. Three years of age is an ideal time to begin teaching responsibility and discipline. Many adults never learned self-discipline and that's one of the reasons we live in a society filled with anger, blame, entitlement, and indulgence. One of parents' most important responsibilities is teaching their children self-discipline and self-responsibility. But what can three-year-olds do? They can take the top off the toothpaste and put it back. They can help make their bed. They can pick up after themselves. They can be taught not to eat too much and why. They can be taught to tell the truth and why. They should be made to do some work and understand why. Then they'll appreciate what they earn. Teach your children the practice of self-control and obedience for their sake as well as yours.

Every action anyone takes has consequences. Whether those consequences are good or bad depends on the action. Children deserve to be taught that when they do things they shouldn't, there are penalties that will increase depending on the seriousness of the offense. We need look no further than our prisons to prove the importance of these lessons. We wouldn't have overcrowded prisons if the people now in them had been taught to be responsible and disciplined when they were between three and seven years of age. In most cases, their parents weren't able to teach them because they hadn't been taught themselves.

There is no excuse for not teaching your children self-discipline and self-responsibility.

Many of today's parents are so concerned about their child getting upset with them or not loving them that they give in to the child's every whim. They buy their children meaningless belongings and, more important, allow them to watch whatever they want on television, on the Internet, or at the movies. There's no curfew, but there's plenty of talking back punctuated with pouting and tantrums. None of those indulgences sends the right message to a child.

Children need, deserve, and want boundaries.

As a parent, it will be your responsibility to know who their friends are and the nature of the homes they visit. If they have access to the Internet, look at their profiles if they use the MySpace.com or Facebook.com services. Have the computer in a common area so you can monitor its use. Be a parent who means what you say. If you tell your children that they will be punished for telling you a lie, you had better punish them. Otherwise, you're teaching them they don't have to do what they say they will do because you don't. How are they to know when you mean something and when you don't if you're inconsistent? If you do what you tell them you're going to do, they'll learn and respect boundaries.

If you always do what you say you're going to do, I can build an empire around you; if you sometimes do what you say you're going to do, you're just another headache for me.

I can't stress enough the magnitude of the statement on the right. You're giving your children a priceless gift when you teach them to make their word their bond before they're seven years old. How many people do you know who always do what they say? Imposing strict discipline will help them all the days of their lives. It's proven that parents who monitor their children's television, music, phone, and computer have fewer problems with them. Children need and want discipline because it tells them you love them and care enough to do the hard job of teaching them right from wrong. Not disciplining children does them a disservice. It's comparable to not telling them boiling water will hurt them and making them learn it for themselves. Our society has become too permissive. Many parents don't discipline themselves or their children. That may explain why we have an obesity problem in America and why American families are deeply in debt. It's time we get back to proven values and the best way to start is with our youth. Parents who set sensible rules have children who are less apt to smoke or take drugs.

1. Turn off the television during meals.
2. Ban music with offensive lyrics.
3. Know where your child is at all times.
4. Impose a curfew.
5. Assign regular chores.
6. Eat dinner together at a regular time.

Begin teaching your children to save when they're five or six. Buy a piggy bank and let them feel how heavy it gets as they save. Show them how saving will provide opportunities when they get older. Teach them how spendthrifts get into debt and actually have less to spend. Open savings accounts for them at age seven and have them make regular deposits. Show them how money can multiply through compound interest. Encourage them to save a percentage of their allowance by matching their savings.

Children are never justified in being disrespectful to anyone, especially their parents. Teach them respect when they're very young and it will carry through the rest of their lives. Don't allow them to be disrespectful or talk back to you. You'll have to scold and discipline them, but always follow it with a confirmation of their value. Every child needs to feel loved, needed, and essential. Don't raise your voice to your children. Teach them you mean business quietly. Don't permit them to yell and scream. Children will always go to the parent who is most lenient and permissive, so be a team and support each other fully in front of the children. If you have a disagreement with your spouse, make sure your work it out in private and never in front of the children. If they see and hear you yelling or raising your voice at each other, it teaches them that is how to deal with problems. Always act as a team when it comes to the children. Show them how Mom and Dad work together and how much they love and support each other so your children emulate that kind of relationship.

PARENTING SUMMARY

Parenting is a difficult job and an enormous responsibility.

1 Children are never justified in being disrespectful to anyone, especially their parents. Begin teaching them responsibility and respect starting at age three.

2. Don't allow them to talk back.

3. Always follow scolding and discipline with a confirmation of their value.

4. Teach your children that they were born to win and deserve to be happy.

5. Teach them they have unlimited possibilities.

6. Teach them to be optimistic and to have faith in themselves.

7. Mean what you say so they learn their boundaries.

8. Don't raise your voice to correct them. Teach them you mean business quietly.

9. Be sure to discipline them only for the wrong acts that they do and not for who they are, never calling them slow, stupid, or anything that reflects on their character.

10. Teach them not to quit and to always do a good job.

11. The best way to instruct is to praise what they do right.

12. Expose them to some faith-based organizations.

13. Make home their place of refuge.

14. Children will always go to the parent who is most

lenient and permissive, so support each other in front of them.

15 Give them love, love, and more love.

QUIZ ANSWERS

● IS THIS PERSON RIGHT FOR YOU?

What your score means:

MOSTLY As: Keep seeing this person and see where it leads—sounds very promising.

MOSTLY Bs: Go on, see where it leads—you never know, things may get even better.

MOSTLY Cs: It's probably time to look for someone who is better suited to you and can make you feel as good as you deserve to.

MOSTLY Ds: No need to break up immediately, but keep your eyes open for someone who might make you feel even better about yourself and your relationship.

● WILL THIS RELATIONSHIP LAST?

What your score means:

If you scored between 15 and 20 points, your chances look good right now—keep on enjoying each other. When you stop having fun together and feeling good about yourself and each other, that's the time to look for someone else.

QUIZ   ANSWERS *(continued)*

If you scored below 15 points, you may want to rethink your relationship. Relationships are all about exploring and learning what it takes to make things work—but if this person doesn't make you feel happy about who you are when you're with him/her, or it might be time to start looking for someone who can. Otherwise, it's hard to make things last.

● CAN YOU SPOT SIGNS OF LOVE-TROUBLE?

What your score means:

If you scored between 10 and 40 points, it might be time to look for a new love. Physical or verbal abuse is never acceptable in a relationship. Jealousy is not really a sign of love. And addictions can start small but usually get worse as time goes on, not better. So if a certain behavior is bothering you now, at the start of a relationship, it will only bother you more as time goes on.

If you scored between 8 and 10 points, even if only a few of these issues make you uncomfortable, it can be a sign of trouble. Opposites might attract, but if you both do not agree on most of the important things and share the values you care about, then it will be hard to weather the storms that every relationship experiences.

If you scored below 7 points, you're off to a good start. There don't seem to be serious warning signs. Keep your eyes open as your relationship progresses, and if something troubles you, speak up. Better now than when it's too late.

5

CAREER AND FINANCE

Your career choice will have ramifications in other areas of your life. My mission in this chapter is to encourage you to think about your options and carefully consider what's most important to you before choosing a career. The first consideration should be: what are you passionate about? Your best career choice will be the one you can't wait to do every day. You'll be at your best doing a job that excites you and one you enjoy learning about.

If you choose a profession you're passionate about, you'll never have to work a day in your life, because you'll be doing what you love to do.

You can have almost any career you desire if you have enough desire, faith, and persistence. The precise steps to attain the career you desire are in chapter 3. The purpose here is to help you determine what's important to you and why.

LIFESTYLE

Lifestyle is an important consideration when selecting a career.

A good way to determine the good life for you is by identifying what you care about most and how much income it requires. You may be someone who has lived in Santa Barbara, California, your entire life and would never consider leaving. In that case, you'll approach your career differently than the person who is willing to move anywhere to further his or her career. How much does lifestyle matter to you? Consider the way you want your life to be twenty-five years from now. Because you have the option of living anywhere in the world, how important is it to you to spend the rest of your life near your family? Do you want your children to go through school in a specific community? Are you interested in making the most money possible, regardless of location? The answers to each of those questions will help you determine your career.

You're the only person who can determine what a good life would be.

COMPENSATION

Consider the compensation of an unskilled worker at $20/hour vs. a professional such as an attorney at $300/hour. It's possible to do the job of an unskilled worker with no prior experience or training. Many people are capable of doing those kinds of jobs. Becoming an attorney requires

Your compensation will be directly related to how easily you can be replaced.

seven years of college. You must specialize in either criminal or civil law. If you choose civil law, additional training is required for your specialty, whether it's divorce law, corporate law, real estate law, etc. Once you have the necessary education and training in a specific area and you understand the rules in a particular state and city, you become very valuable and hard to replace. Across the entire job market, you'll find the same large

In sales, those on commission can make a lot more money than those on salary.

spread in compensation based on supply and demand. Painters make less money than electricians. Taxi drivers make less money than computer technicians. If you want to make the most money possible and have job security, make sure you go into a field where you will be very valuable and hard to replace.

In my former real estate company, all sales people were paid based on straight commission, which carries some risk. Our top earners made between one million and five million dollars a year and no one earned less than two hundred thousand dollars. A less risky salaried job in the same field pays no more than one hundred and fifty thousand dollars. Think through how much risk you're willing to take if you want to make a great deal of money.

If your goal is making the most money you can, you'll need to live where the money is—cities like New York, Los Angeles, San Francisco, Boston, Chicago, Dallas, and Houston. It's hard to find the same opportunities in smaller cities. If your objective is maximizing income, your location options will be limited.

You may be willing to make less money to live in your ideal location. In that case, you'll have few restrictions and can think in terms of small coastal towns like Carmel, Newport Beach, La Jolla, and Santa Barbara in California or Boca Raton, Myrtle Beach, and Cape Cod on the East Coast. You can even consider exotic locations like Italy, New Zealand, or Tahiti. You can live in a perfect climate with smog-free air and no freeways or crowds. If location is your primary concern, your career fields may include government, medicine, tourism, or small business.

There's no right or wrong choice—it's a matter of your desired lifestyle.

QUIZ	**WHAT KIND OF JOB SHOULD YOU HAVE?**

1 What's the most important aspect of a career for you?

  a Salary.
  b Enjoying what I'm doing.
  c Where I live.

2 You would want to work where you . . .

  a Get to be creative—like in entertainment or the arts.
  b Work with something concrete like numbers or in science.
  c Manage or work closely with others.

3 Your ideal office would be . . .

  a In a skyscraper corner office with lots of space.
  b Where I could wear my PJs—home!
  c In an office with my coworkers.

4 Where do you want to live?

  a Some place with a strong community, like a suburb.
  b A big metropolis; New York City or L.A. would be cool.

| QUIZ | **WHAT KIND OF JOB SHOULD YOU HAVE?** *(continued)* |

c Some place with a lot of culture or history, like Nashville or Austin.

5 How many hours do you want to put in?

a Overtime is fine, as long as I have enough time for a life.

b If it makes me a lot of money, the more the merrier.

c As long as I love what I'm doing, and it doesn't feel like I'm working, it doesn't matter.

| SCORE | Count up your points, then flip to the end of the chapter to find out what your score means. |

1 a. 3; b. 1; c. 2   **4** a. 2; b. 3; c. 1

2 a. 1; b. 3; c. 2   **5** a. 2; b. 3; c. 1

3 a. 3; b. 1; c. 2

BIGGER IS USUALLY NOT BETTER

To increase your peace of mind and minimize your stress, it's important to learn that bigger is generally not better. It isn't that you don't want a new home, new car, or certain luxuries; you just need to understand that more and bigger usually don't bring happiness. Comfortable, convenient, and practical make the most sense. Don't envy the people living in the 10,000-square-foot house.

Ask yourself if your meals will taste better if your dining room is the size of a basketball court or if the food is served on gold plates? How many rooms do you need? Will an especially large bedroom make you sleep any better? What good is a ten-car garage? How many cars do you want to drive and maintain? Having more than you need does you no good and can be harmful. To enjoy financial success, practice restraint and moderation. When considering your dream home, think in terms of how much you will use. You'll most likely discover that about 2,500 square feet is adequate. There are a variety of benefits of choosing this option vs. the 10,000-square-foot home:

All that glitters is not gold.

1. The house will cost you one-third as much.
2. You can pay it off three times faster.
3. Your insurance, utilities, taxes, maintenance, and furnishings will all cost a fraction of what they would be for the larger house.

④ When you're ready to sell, there will be more potential buyers.

Forget the Joneses and let them keep up with themselves.

Here are some proven methods to increase your success in business:

❶ Come in early and stay late. Employers value, give raises to, and promote people who show initiative and dedication.

❷ Do what's asked without reservation or complaint. Do more than you're paid to do and you'll be rewarded. Never say, "It's not my job."

❸ Winners complete each task as soon as possible. Become known as the person who makes things happen in a timely fashion.

❹ Be meticulous. Attention to detail is uncommon. You'll stand out by doing your tasks with precision. People judge you by the neatness and cleanliness of your dress, car, office, and home. Being orderly in these areas reveals the way you handle other responsibilities in your life.

❺ Treat your company as if it were your own. By approaching your work as if you owned the company, you pay attention to the small things like being prudent with your expense account, not wasting time, restricting your phone calls to business, turning off lights, and not wasting supplies. Employers notice and reward such behaviors.

If you buy more than you need today, you may not be able to buy what you need tomorrow.

6 **Responsiveness is a highly visible virtue.** Get in the habit of responding to people immediately. Even if you aren't able to do what they want right away, you can email or call them and let them know you got the message and are on the case.

7 **Make your word your bond.** People who always do what they say are rarer than rainbows. You acquire this habit by learning to be careful what you commit to and watching what you say. If you say you'll meet someone at 8:00 P.M., that doesn't mean 8:05. If you say you'll see them at the game tonight, be there every time. Become someone who consistently does exactly what you say you will do. By this act alone, others will soon learn they can depend on you, and your career and social life will soar.

8 **Under-commit and over-deliver.** The common practice today is over-committing and under-delivering. Items usually cost more than

estimated and take longer to receive than you've been told. Be the person who completes the task early and under budget. Exceed your employer's expectations and you'll be the one moving up the ladder of success. This practice is equally beneficial in your personal life.

9 **Acknowledge people's virtues**. Build up your fellow employees. You're evaluated by the way you speak of others, particularly when they're not present. Be the person who refuses to gossip or criticize.

10 **Be decisive.** A common trait of leaders and successful people is decisiveness. Take your time gathering the facts, but once you have them, make your decision and be slow to change it. Don't second-guess yourself.

11 **Practice win–win.** You'll develop an enviable reputation by making each situation you're involved in fair to all concerned. For instance, say you're a real estate agent and meet with someone who wants sell her home. She's considering giving you the listing and tells you she wants to price her home at $330,000. You're an expert in their market and know the home can sell for $380,000. It may be tempting to take the listing at her price to make a quick commission. If you did that, you wouldn't have a win–win situation because the owner would eventually learn that you had taken advantage of her. She would not do business with you again and may spread the word about your lack of integrity. By taking the high road and telling her you could get the higher price, you would still make your commission and have a client who will likely recommend you to other homeowners. The moral road is always the best choice. My mentor used to say, "If a deal has any smell to it, stay away from it." He also told me to "Always play the game straight down the middle." His philosophy was to be very careful about the road you choose because there's a good chance you may have to make a return trip. Make sure any deal you're a part of is good for all concerned. Don't be afraid to leave a little on the table and never try and get the last dollar.

12 **Be the master of your destiny.** Make your own decisions. It's wise to ask for professional advice in areas in which you don't have expertise, but you still need to make the final decision. No one else thinks exactly like you or knows what's right for you.

13 **To be a success, you must differ from the majority.** If you're like everyone else, you can't be outstanding. Be different in your attitudes and actions. You'll stand out if you're the thoughtful one doing acts of kindness for your co-workers. You'll be unusual if you're the one who cheers up the people who are down, lends a helping hand, wears a warm smile, and has a consistently affirmative attitude. Be the one who refuses to gossip, doesn't spread rumors, and refuses to be irritable or mean-spirited.

⑭ **Don't be defensive.** Be quick to admit it when you make a mistake.

FINANCE

Sound financial management improves your peace of mind and lessens your stress. My mentor taught me:

Economics comes after breathing.

You need money to satisfy your basic living requirements, acquire the possessions you desire, help people you love, and be able to indulge in the activities of your choice. Having sufficient money will be determined more by how much you keep than by how much you make. Some people make a lot of money and have nothing left at the end of the year.

Then there are those who make far less money, yet save more than the higher earner. Most Americans live beyond their means, spending all they make and then going into debt.

Intelligent financial management requires minimizing debt. In the beginning, some debt may be necessary for large purchases like a home. A reasonable goal is having no mortgage on your home by age *Spend less than you make.* fifty. You should pay cash for most of the things you can afford. Debt gives someone else control over your life. Learn to live on 80 percent of what you earn, put 10 percent into a balanced investment portfolio, and keep the other 10 percent in a money-market account as an emergency fund until you have the equivalent of six months' worth of living expenses.

Credit card companies compete for your business by making it *Borrowing money isn't as difficult as paying it back.* effortless to get their cards. This is another example of how getting in is easy. Interest rates soar when the borrower doesn't pay the monthly bill in full. Rates as high as 20 percent are not uncommon. The penalties are severe if you fall behind on your payments. Excessive debt is a huge problem for Americans and you don't want to suffer this fate. If you use a credit card, be sure you pay the entire balance each month.

RESERVES

Establish an emergency fund before starting to invest. I recommend a minimum of three months' worth of living expenses. The larger your reserves, the more peace you'll have and the better position you'll be in to take advantage of bargains. Opportunity will come knocking throughout your life—often at the most unexpected times.

A secret to success is being ready for your opportunities when they come.

The smart way to be prepared is having cash reserves, as well as the ability to get money when you need it. In reviewing my financial life, I recognize that much of my success came from being able to take advantage of opportunities when they presented themselves.

MORTGAGES

Financial markets fluctuate from one extreme to the other. In the past twenty years, interest rates have been as high as 21 percent and as low as 2 percent. Because of those extremes, I advise caution when borrowing. Lenders promote variable-rate mortgages because they have attractive starting rates, but they also represent the highest risk. Variable-rate mortgages are yet another example of something that's easy to get into, but hard to get out of and risky. Seek the counsel of a knowledgeable professional on mortgages who will give you unbiased advice before making a home loan. If you select a variable-rate mortgage, ensure that the rate is capped (meaning there is a limit

You make your profit when you buy, not when you sell.

on how high the rate can go) and that you can make the payments should it rise to the highest point. You'll have less risk and more peace of mind with a fixed-rate, fully amortized mortgage.

BUY RIGHT

This is not a commonly known concept, but it is one that can greatly improve your future if you implement it. You want to become skillful and determined about buying right. With any large purchase, ask yourself: *could I make a profit if I had to sell this item the next day?* If you buy a new car, you can't get back what you paid for it if you had to sell it the next day. A well-selected used car is almost always a better financial choice. You'll make your most profitable buys from someone who must sell. There are bargains to be found because of deaths, foreclosures, divorces, bankruptcies, and job transfers. Patience and research are necessary to buy right. If you buy a home right, you can sell it in a short time for a profit. An excellent way to ensure a profit on the purchase of your first home is buying at a foreclosure sale. With patience, you can buy a home for 60–70 percent of current value at foreclosure. You'll need the help of a real estate agent knowledgeable in foreclosures to protect your interests. People who are buying at or above market and hoping for an increase in value put themselves in peril.

| QUIZ | ARE YOU A SPENDER OR A SAVER? |

1 When I go shopping, I usually find something that's on my list—and sometimes one or two other things I could use, too.

a Agree.
b Disagree.

2 If I won $1 million in the lottery, I would . . .

a Go out and buy everything I've ever wanted: a car and vacations for me and all my friends. With that kind of money, why worry?
b I'd go out on a great shopping spree but I wouldn't buy anything really big until I got some advice.

3 If the money in my bank account goes down to $5, I . . .

   a Get really nervous and only write checks in an emergency.

   b Don't worry because I can still use my credit card for whatever I want—that's what it's there for.

4 If I see something I like, I . . .

   a Only buy it if it's on sale or if it seems like a good buy, even if it means wasting time and coming back another time.

   b Buy it—it would be a waste of time to have to come back later and I may never be able to find it again.

5 I like to use my money to have a good time and enjoy life—what else is money for?

   a Agree.

   b Disagree.

SCORE	Count up your points, then flip to the end of the chapter to find out what your score means.

1 a. 2; b. 1.   **4** a. 1; b. 2

2 a. 2; b. 1   **5** a. 2; b. 1

3 a. 1; b. 2

TAKING RISK

Most aspects of life involve risk; therefore, it's important to learn when and how much risk to take. Life's

*Never risk more than
you can afford to lose.*
precarious enough without know-
ingly putting yourself in jeopardy. If
you're choosing who to marry, you'll

want to take as little risk as possible because the consequences of a mistake are severe. An important rule
for acquiring wealth is protecting your capital. It's
one thing to lose the profit you planned to make and
another to lose your capital. Protecting what you've
acquired is often harder than getting it.

Risk and reward are closely tied together. Make
sure that the greater risk you take, the higher the
reward. One of the best times to bet on yourself is
before having a family. This is when you can afford
to take reasonable chances. Believe in yourself and
realize that quantum leaps are possible. If you want
to buy a risky stock, only buy the amount you can
afford to lose should the company go broke.

Slow and steady does win the financial race, so
move cautiously forward without going backward
and you'll acquire more wealth in the long run. As
I said before, a key ingredient to financial success is
being able to take advantage of opportunities when

they appear and that usually requires capital. If you
don't have the capital and find an outstanding opportunity, there are always investors ready to put up the
money for a percentage of the deal. Seizing opportunities is one of the best and safest
ways to get a good financial start.

Foreclosures are an excellent
example of a good opportunity. All
properties that are being foreclosed

*Finding good
opportunities is a
great deal harder than
finding the money.*

on must be advertised in the local paper for a certain
period of time. It requires no money to find foreclosures, determine if they are good properties, get the
loan information, and decide what you are willing
to bid at auction. When you discover a property that
has loans that are well below market value, you'll have
no difficulty finding someone to put up the money.
One of the reasons foreclosures present a good opportunity is they require a cashier's check for the full
purchase price at the time of the auction and most
people don't have that kind of ready cash. The people
who have the money aren't usually interested in going
through what's necessary to find and rehab the good
deals. That combination spells opportunity for the
hard-working young person who's willing to do the
research to find the good deals and then oversee the
renovation. We made $200,000 on one deal in less

than three months by buying and fixing up a foreclosure and so can you.

AVOID IMPORTANT DECISIONS WHEN FEELING TOO HIGH OR TOO LOW

Don't make important financial decisions when you're feeling high or low because your judgment might be clouded. When anxiety steps in, good judgment steps out; when you're euphoric, you don't see things clearly. When you're feeling low, remember what it was like when you were on a high and vice versa. If you're feeling desperate or invincible, seek professional financial advice before making important decisions.

There's never a time to be careless in financial matters.

It's natural to use caution when you don't have much money and you're about to risk some of it. I've found that it's also easy to make a foolish decision when you're flush with money. If you purchase 1,000 shares of stock at $5 a share and sell it a week later for $10 a share, making a tidy $5,000 profit in that week, it's natural to think you should buy 5,000 shares next time so you can make five times as much. I've fallen into this trap several times and each time it's caused me immense pain.

I bought 5,000 shares of a stock for $2 a share a few years ago based on a tip from a close friend who had done his research and believed strongly in the company. The first week I owned the stock it went from $2 to $24 per share, giving me a gain of $110,000. I was feeling great and immediately bought 20,000 shares at $24, expecting the stock to continue its climb. Two weeks later, the stock dropped back to $5 per share; four years later, it was still at that level. I eventually sold the stock and took a loss of $365,000. Oh, how I wish I'd had the good judgment to be happy with my $110,000 profit. Never be greedy. Be thankful when you make a profit and be sure to take it.

BECOME A CONTRARIAN

One of the most beneficial lessons I've ever learned is to be a contrarian. When everyone else is buying, you should be selling and when they are selling, you should be buying. That advice has helped me make and keep a great deal of money. Being a contrarian saved my family more than one million dollars in the rising stock market in the year 2000. People with no financial experience were advising what stocks to buy and borrowing money to buy them. No matter what stock anyone bought, they seemed to make money. I had learned that anything that goes up too fast is going to come down. Most people were in a buying frenzy and my wife suggested we sell a large portion of our stocks. The market soon crashed and even the blue-chip companies lost up to half their value. Those who borrowed money to buy stocks lost what they borrowed and some had no means of repayment. Companies and individuals went bankrupt. This was the time of the Enron, WorldCom, and Tyco scandals. Within a year, stocks were depressed and so was the economy. Most people started selling, so we started buying. Those stocks have continued to rise over the past five years and are now worth twice what we paid for them.

Here are a few significant suggestions when it comes to investing:

1. Don't borrow money for any risky investment unless you can afford to lose it.
2. Don't put all your investment funds in any single category such as stocks. Diversify with real estate, annuities, bonds, and money-market accounts.
3. When a market gets red hot and has gone up fast, start taking some profits and building up cash.
4. When a market has gone down drastically, sit on the sidelines until it starts back up and then begin to buy selectively.

The same philosophy holds true for the real estate market. In 2006, housing prices were at an all-time high and people were caught up in buying fever. People got into bidding contests and paid more than the asking price. Most people were buying, so we sold most of our holdings. In less than a year, the housing market hit the skids. Those

Become a contrarian if you want to make money.

who bought at the top of the market could not sell their homes without large losses and the number of foreclosures doubled. Most began trying to sell, so it was again time to buy. I've watched this pattern play out for more than thirty years.

Don't try and find the exact bottom or top of a market—it can be elusive. Be satisfied buying or selling near either extreme. If a deal seems too good to be true, it almost always is, so use extra caution.

Doing the opposite of the many also works well in other areas of life. If there's a movie premiere and there are lines at the theater on opening day, you're better off seeing it a week later. You'll have no parking problems, you'll find the best seats, and there will be no crowd at the snack bar. If most people are flying home the day after Christmas, you're wise to wait an extra day. The airports will be less crowded, the tickets may cost less, you'll get through security faster, the planes will not be as full, and they are more likely to be on time. If you want less stress and a richer life, make it your practice to be a contrarian.

Estimate your income and expenses for the coming year and then keep an accurate record of the actual amounts, making any sacrifices needed to ensure you take in more than you spend. Save enough to pay your taxes at year's end and make it a practice to overestimate the taxes so you're not caught short. People and their taxes have produced many sad tales. Not long ago, a famous singer was facing prison for back taxes. He spent several years playing additional concerts to settle his debt with the IRS. You never want to get behind on your taxes because the penalties are severe and the IRS is relentless in collecting. Keep good records of your net worth (assets minus liabilities) annually and make sure it's increasing.

If you want financial peace of mind, make it a practice to live below your means.

By *living below your means* I mean you should make it your rule to buy less than you can afford. Make it a habit not to pay for goods or services before you receive them. If you have to stretch to buy a $15,000 car, buy one for $10,000. You will never regret adopting this philosophy. Any permanent overhead (recurring expenses) is a serious responsibility, so make your choices with care. For example, you'll learn that the cost of a swimming pool will be less than the cost of its maintenance over time. One-time expenses are safer and less painful than recurring ones. Buying a bicycle is a one-time expense, whereas buying a horse is just the beginning of the story. You must then feed it, board it, keep it in good health, and buy all that is needed to ride and care for it. Make it a habit not to pay for goods or services before you receive them.

You can dry up the Pacific Ocean if you keep taking out more water than you're putting in. Sound financial management means spending less than you make. As you start to succeed financially, develop a second source of income to supplement your salary. This will likely include investments in stocks, bonds, and real estate, all of which can be income-producing. Tax-free municipal bonds are one of the safest investments you can make. A reputable financial advisor can be of great help.

You are the creator of your own fate and the master of your destiny.

The people who fail to accumulate money are often easily swayed by the opinion of others. Only listen to those who have your best interest at heart and a proven track record in financial success and then make the final decisions yourself.

You can't blame anyone else for what happens in your life. That's why it's important for you to have the final say about every decision. If you practice what's been advocated here, you'll succeed. Once you're successful, keep your success private because the scam artists are searching for those careless enough to flaunt their wealth.

To become a financial success, you'll need to harness the wild steed of desire.

QUIZ   HOW BIG A RISK-TAKER ARE YOU?

1 If I had enough money to live on for a year, right now, I'd . . .

   a Quit my job and take off for a year because I may never get that chance again.

   b Keep working and spend the extra cash on fun stuff.

   c Try to save most of it.

2 I would change jobs if . . .

   a I thought the new job would be something I would like to do more and would be much better at.

   b The new job title would sound cool to my friends, even though the money is no better.

   c The new place offered me more money, even if I didn't really like the job.

3 I envy people who are richer than I am and I want to be one of them one day.

- **a** Strongly agree.
- **b** Not sure.
- **c** Disagree.

4 I planned a great vacation and then find out I lost my job. I . . .

- **a** Go anyway because I figure I'll feel more like looking for a new job after I've had some fun.
- **b** Go on a vacation that doesn't cost as much but still will be fun.
- **c** Cancel the vacation plans and start job-hunting.

5 Here's how I feel about debt:

- **a** All my friends have some, for college loans and stuff, so it doesn't bother me.
- **b** I don't want to have credit card debt but I realize that sometimes that's what happens in life.
- **c** I don't like the idea of owing anybody anything.

6 If I see something I like, I . . .

- **a** Try to talk myself out of it because I often regret buying stuff afterward.
- **b** Shop around to see if other stores have the same thing for less.
- **c** Buy it—it's not worth the time to come back later and it might be gone by then.

QUIZ	**HOW BIG A RISK-TAKER ARE YOU?** *(continued)*

7 When I am facing a big money decision, I . . .

- **a** Do some research on the Internet, call friends, and even see what my parents or some other expert-types have to say.
- **b** Call my friends to see what they would do.
- **c** Flip a coin—these things even out.

SCORE	Count up your points, then flip to the end of the chapter to find out what your score means.

1 a. 3; b. 2; c. 1   **5** a. 3; b. 2; c. 1

2 a. 1; b. 2; c. 3   **6** a. 1; b. 2; c. 3

3 a. 3; b. 2; c. 1   **7** a. 1; b. 2; c. 3

4 a. 3; b. 2; c. 1

To build your financial future, you need money working for you. You can't carelessly spend and save at the same time. Consider every dollar you make as your personal little money machine. If you save the dollar, it will keep working for you and, like a well-fed rabbit, it can multiply over and over. Every dollar you spend is gone forever. Money will not bring happiness, but it will make your journey through life more pleasant.

Many young people feel luck can determine their destiny. Your destiny will not be determined by luck. Luck is arbitrary—it happens by chance. Sometimes we see people have good fortune, but that is very different from luck. Know from this day forward that your future is in your own hands and you sure don't want to depend on happenstance to determine it.

① Study and learn about your profession.
② Work hard and smart.
③ Save for a rainy day.
④ Invest your money wisely.
⑤ Never risk more than you can afford to lose.
⑥ Make each situation you're in a win–win.
⑦ Go the extra mile.
⑧ Under-promise and over-deliver.

If you follow all of these rules, you won't have to worry about luck and any good fortune that comes your way will simply be a bonus.

Remember that it's not what money can do *for* you, but what you can do *with* it. Your financial success will help you live a productive life and allow you the opportunity of blessing others. Getting in position to be a blessing to others will turn out to be a gift to you. The greatest joy I've found is being able to help others make their dreams come true. If you build your wealth steadily, you and your family will be able to enjoy a wonderful life and have the ability to help whoever you choose as your bonus.

QUIZ **ANSWERS**

● **WHAT KIND OF JOB SHOULD YOU HAVE?**

What your score means:

If you scored between 12 and 15 points, you want to be big-time and live the high-life, with spacious offices and a job that pays well, even if you have to work a lot. A career in finances or in science might suit you, or a business that lets you climb the ladder to being a boss.

If you scored between 8 and 11 points, you're a people person who loves that human interaction. Where you live and your surroundings are important to you. Jobs in sales, politics, and real estate might appeal to you.

If you scored between 5 and 7 points, salary isn't as important to you as your passions and freedom. You don't mind working a lot as long as you love your job. If you want to go into something more creative and more flexible, try entertainment, art, or advertising.

● ARE YOU A SPENDER OR A SAVER?

What your score means:

If you scored between 9 and 10 points, you're a Spender—you know how to have a good time. But even if you wind up earning a lot of money, it's a good idea to think about how you can save a little as you go or you could find yourself in some serious debt before long.

If you scored between 6 and 8 points, you're a good balance between a Spender and a Saver—not too impulsive and not too worried. You recognize that money is a tool for the lifestyle you want. So keep on thinking before you spend, and trying to save a little every paycheck.

If you scored below 5 points, you're a Saver—that's great because it will help you be prepared for the ups and downs in life. But remind yourself not to worry too much—and allow yourself to have a little splurge every now and then.

● HOW BIG A RISK-TAKER ARE YOU?

What your score means:

If you scored between 19 and 21 points, you are willing to take a lot of risks. Sometimes risks pay off—but if you don't also start trying to weigh your choices more carefully, you could find yourself in financial trouble.

If you scored between 11 and 18 points, you seem able to balance some risk with common sense. That's just what you'll need to succeed in your career.

If you scored between 7 and 10 points, you don't seem comfortable taking a lot of risks. While you don't want to play it completely safe all your life, you're probably on the right path to financial security.

6

LOVE AND TRUTH

I t was the winter of 1945 and no one knew it yet, but World War II would be ending soon. I was living in Miami with my mom, who had given birth to me when she was only sixteen. My dad had joined the Navy and been sent to the Pacific Theater to do battle with the Japanese. One day, he received a letter from my mom, stating that she wanted a divorce. In those days, a woman needed her husband's consent for a divorce to be legal. He wrote back that the only way he would consent was for her to deliver me to his mother in Macon, Georgia, and sign papers that she would never see me again. She did as he requested.

My grandmother took good care of me. When I was four, my dad, who had remarried, came to get me, but my grandmother refused to give me up. She said she had agreed to raise me and that was what she intended to do. My dad drove up from Florida and visited me from time to time. Over the next six years, my step-mom gave him three more sons. My dad would occasionally ask his mother to let me live with them, but each time she refused.

In the early 1950s, she developed breast cancer and passed away at the age of fifty-four. After she passed away, I was moved from Macon to Jacksonville, Florida, to live with my dad, step-mom, and three brothers. I was excited that I was going to be living with my dad, but little did I know what lay ahead. The first few weeks in my new environment shocked me.

I'd been spoiled by my grandmother and was utterly unprepared for a military environment. I was instructed to say "Yes, sir" and "Yes, ma'am" when addressing any adults. I was told I would share a bedroom, make my own bed, help with the dishes, and help clean the house. I was told if I wanted spending money I would need to baby-sit or cut lawns to earn it. I had to go to bed and get up at a certain time and was required to ask permission for almost anything I wanted to do. That was a lot for a twelve-year-old to absorb.

When I was with my grandmother, I'd lived ten years in the same house, but from the time I moved in with my dad, it seemed we never stopped moving. I went to live with my new family in Jacksonville, Florida, and we were soon transferred to Miramar Naval Air Station in San Diego. Soon, we were on our way to a shipyard in Norfolk, Virginia. Less than a year later, we were headed back across the United States to a Navy base in Alameda, California, and six months later back across the country to Memphis, Tennessee. Eight months later, we were on our way to Point Mugu Naval Air Station near Oxnard, California. My last stop with them was Escondido, California, where I graduated from high school and set out on my own when my dad and the rest of the family transferred to Rhoda, Spain. I had attended three different high schools in four years.

Once again, what looked like a huge setback in my life turned out to be a blessing. These new experiences were exactly what I needed and they were done in love. I was taught honesty and truth in no uncertain terms. I needed discipline and I got it. I needed to learn to share and I did. Learn not to judge things as good or bad when they occur. Wait and see what happens.

It was often unsettling to grow up never knowing my mother. It was hard watching sports stars saying "Hi, Mom" when they were interviewed on television.

I felt abandoned and hurt from time to time. Occasionally, I would think about trying to find my mom, but usually the impulse passed as I concluded she could easily find me if she had the desire. I wanted to know what kind of a woman she was and how I was different from my step-brothers. I wanted to know if I had any other siblings. Many more years passed and all I had was several pictures of her. My aunt told me a few things but didn't know what became of her after she left me with my grandmother.

One day a couple years ago, my daughter Shirley asked if I ever wondered about my mom and I said I did. She asked if she could try and find her for me. I said, "Of course," but thought there was no chance she'd succeed. Shirley then asked her mother, my former wife Patricia, to help her. At this time, I had not seen or heard from my mom in sixty years. Less than two weeks later, I got an email from Patricia telling me she had found my sister. Since then, my sister and I have communicated on a regular basis and I have learned all the things I wanted to know about my mom. She passed away at a very young age in 1980. She had four more children, three girls and a boy, who I now know as my half-sisters and -brother. My mom was a quiet person, an excellent cook and mother, and loved to fish. When I was moved to

Florida to live with my dad, I did not know it, but I was only a few miles from where my mom was living. Her children adored her and she had a reputation for always helping others and never complaining. I now know she was a wonderful, caring woman. My sister, Teresa Whelan, has been one of the great joys of my life. She lives near Dallas and has eight children of her own. She and her husband of thirty-seven years, Mike, will be coming to visit us here on the Big Island this year.

We are about to embark on our final and perhaps most important chapter, "Love and Truth." The story you have just read is about love and truth: love from so many family members throughout my life and then finding out the truth about my mom. There can be no two subjects worth your attention more than the two you are about to encounter.

In this chapter, I'll discuss the most valuable concepts I've ever studied. Like me, you may not fully appreciate this philosophy at first, but as you continue learning, your understanding will grow. It amazes me that I can read something and feel confident that I understand it and read the same words four years later and see them in a new light. As we develop, we see the world differently and the things we learned take on new significance.

The more you live love and truth, the more content, prosperous, and joyful your life will become. Ethical behavior helps you avoid conflict. In the following pages, you'll learn the foolishness of worry, doubt, and fear and how to minimize them. You'll be given concepts to help you think more clearly, improve relationships, use better judgment, and increase your self-respect.

Love and truth are the foundation of all that is good.

Learning human relations and habits as discussed in earlier chapters is straightforward and uncomplicated if accompanied by desire and determination. They are necessary building blocks for your success. The philosophies you're about to study are more intricate and difficult to master. As you apply them, your life will steadily improve.

I've studied the concepts you're about to learn for more than twenty years and will continue studying them the rest of my life. I've discovered that the more I practice these teachings, the better my life becomes. As my understanding improves, I find there's more to learn. For example, I'm working on the practice of unconditional love and it's been quite a challenge. To love unconditionally was a strange concept at first. There were a few people I loved in this manner, people I knew I'd always love no matter what they did. My new goal is to develop unconditional love for all mankind. I've improved although I continually fall short of the mark. Some of the attributes of love are humility, kindness, understanding, and compassion. When I find myself impatient, aggravated, or arrogant, I recognize I have a long way to go. To acquire the virtues discussed in this chapter requires a strong desire coupled with persistence and effort.

> *Love and truth are the two most significant virtues in the world.*

As you adopt love and truth and put them into action, you'll experience a life most only dream about. My goal in this chapter is to inspire you.

QUIZ   HOW THOUGHTFUL ARE YOU?

1 When you are looking for a significant other, you usually look for someone who is . . .

a Supportive and caring. If he/she is a little easy on the eyes, though, it doesn't hurt.

b Fun and adventurous. I need to be entertained and just want someone to have fun with.

c Good-looking. Appearance is what initially attracts people, so I can't help but go for someone I think is hot, but he/she has to have a personality I can get along with, too.

QUIZ	**HOW THOUGHTFUL ARE YOU?** *(continued)*

2 You think community service is . . .

  a Something I'm planning on doing, but can't seem to find the time.

  b A good thing and I try to fit it in whenever I can.

  c Fulfilling. I can't imagine my life without it.

3 You and your friends have been hanging out in your living room, and when they leave, you realize it's a pigsty. You . . .

  a Pick up the big stuff so it doesn't look so bad and your parents won't nag you.

  b Clean it so it looks better than before. You hate messes.

  c Leave it. But only because you really don't think your parents will care.

4 At school, you see the social "outcast" being teased. You . . .

  a Say something like, "Come on, guys." I don't understand why people are so mean.

  b Ignore it. If I say something, I might make the situation worse.

  c Stop and ask the person being picked on if he wants to walk to class with me.

5 You and your friend have been planning on going to a concert for months, and three days before, your crush asks you to go. You . . .

a Tell my crush sorry—I already have plans.

b Tell my friend I have a family thing that night. I know it may not be right, but my crush may get the wrong impression if I say I can't go.

c Explain the situation to my friend and hope she understands. If she seems really upset, I won't back out on my plans.

SCORE | Count up your points, then flip to the end of the chapter to find out what your score means.

1 a. 3; b. 2; c. 1   **4** a. 2; b. 1; c. 3

2 a. 1; b. 2; c. 3   **5** a. 3; b. 1; c. 2

3 a. 2; b. 3; c. 1

LOVE

Love is the most important word and virtue in any language. It is the secret to peace, happiness, and success. Love can warm the coldest heart. If you have no other quality, you can succeed with love. Without it, you will fail.

Jesus taught that the most important virtues are faith, hope, and love, but the greatest of these is love.

Love is giving of one's self without any thought of anything in return.

Considering what's required to live up to those definitions, it's clear why love is hard to find. Here are some of the most common reasons given for loving someone: he or she is attractive, smart, passionate, sophisticated, rich, famous, fun, or sexy. Those attributes have nothing to do with love.

Relationships demand unconditional acceptance and mutual selflessness.

Conditional love is not love. You love because you want to and for no other reason. Even if the object of your love resists, you still have the right and responsibility to love him or her. There's no defense for love and it helps free you from the weight and pain of the world. Love is spiritual and never harmful. A manifestation of love is bliss.

Love is about how I can serve, not what's in it for me.

Love is frequently found when you least expect it. Let everything you say be an expression of the beauty in your heart. All creatures need love. Love is kind and comforts like the sunshine after rain. Only in love can one and one still equal one. Love's the magic that transforms all things into strength and beauty. Memories of love live on in the hearts and souls of those who were loved. You never forget the feelings of your first love or the love of a deceased grandparent. Love is based on respect. Love sees with faultless vision and is its own reward, its own joy, and its own satisfaction. Love leads to justice, freedom, and forgiveness.

Think, speak, and act lovingly and your every need will be supplied.

When you have the eyes of love, you see love everywhere. As you practice love, your life becomes controlled by your heart and not your head. The heart is happiest when it beats for others. Be generous with your love and you'll be loved and revered. There are many ways to express happiness, but there's only one way to find it and that's through love.

LOVE OF SELF MUST PRECEDE SELFLESS LOVE

You'll find joy and lasting happiness when you serve others and the added benefit is self-love. When you only please yourself, you won't experience self-love and therefore you will not be able to love others. The rewards of developing self-love are incredible. I could have saved myself from much anxiety, guilt, and regret had I followed this advice. Now I see that selfishness and self-indulgence block the pathway to self-love.

Much of my dating was in pursuit of self-gratification and not the benefit and welfare of my date. When I left my family, I was only thinking of myself. Putting others first doesn't come naturally. Given that love is life's greatest experience, why should you wait any longer? Put aside your selfishness and greed, replacing them with love for others and generosity, and enter a world of joy and blessedness.

As long as you're greatly influenced by the opinions of others, you'll never be free.

Love doesn't come to you; it comes from inside you. Loving yourself is a by-product of doing the things you know you should do. You develop self-love as you focus on others, and become humble, thoughtful, forgiving, generous, and compassionate. When your self-love is strong, you won't be bothered by other people's opinions.

As your self-love increases, you'll experience peace, joy, confidence, and self-esteem. Other people who know how to love will be drawn to you and your life will become the best it's ever been.

LOVE FOR ALL

A decent and worthy goal is love for all mankind and all living things. You're living love when you have compassion for those who hate, slander, or condemn you. This may sound odd or not make sense to you without further explanation. By exhibiting goodwill toward your enemies, you gain strength by leaving meanness and revenge behind. You demonstrate wisdom, perceiving that those who hate or want to hurt others are living in ignorance. You understand

You know that those who hate or hurt others will pay a high price, so you have compassion for them.

they will suffer until they learn the consequences of their thoughts and actions. Understanding love has shown you that all forms of hatred lead to cruelty and self-destruction.

One reason it's difficult to live love is the emphasis we place on competition. Americans compete in sports, school, and business. We experience competition for mates and social status. You can't rejoice when a competitor is injured and think you're living love. It's easy to be a winner, but how do you respond when you lose? When living love, you still want to win, but you're honestly gracious when you lose. We're in this world together, each having the need to feel important, wanted, and needed. Sometimes we need to be cheered and other times we need to do the cheering.

By letting go of hatred, prejudice, cynicism and intolerance, you'll experience improved relationships, like yourself better, and enjoy less stress and a new level of serenity. Living love takes practice, just like any other disposition you've acquired. You learn to do it one day and one person at a time.

SELFLESS LOVE

Around 555 B.C., Buddha said, "No self, no problem." By practicing that concept, I've realized the enormity of those few words. In my view, this means getting our focus off ourselves. You can do it by eliminating lust, pride, self-indulgence, hatred, self-pity, and vanity. As children, we learned the concept of *me* and *mine*. Instead of being taught selflessness, we grew up thinking we were all that mattered and our world was the only world. Our questions were all alike: *what am I going to get for my birthday? For Christmas? Can I go to camp? When can I have a bicycle? When do I get a car?* For our first twelve to fifteen years, the only two people who mattered were *I* and *me*. It's not easy to go from that paradigm to selfless love.

What we aren't taught early in life is the pain and agony that follow selfishness.

This is your chance to save yourself from grief by learning the joys and rewards of selflessness and the agony and penalties of selfishness. To understand *no self, no problem,* you need look no further than your next perceived problem. As you assess the situation, you'll discover that each of your problems revolves around you being inconvenienced. If your meal isn't ready on time, your car won't start, you can't get the date you want, or an accident closes down the highway, you feel you have a problem. Once you eliminate the "Oh, poor me" syndrome, you'll see there's no problem. Get over your preoccupation with self and the problems dissolve. Learn to accept what is without complaint. Keep your attitude upbeat. Remind yourself that today's misfortune or sadness carries within it the seeds of tomorrow's joy. If you don't like a situation, decide how you want it to be and then set out making it that way. You'll have less stress and a more pleasant life by adopting this attitude.

Each self-seeking act leads to suffering.

As you practice selflessness, your patience improves, your anger diminishes, and your frustrations pass. As you move toward selfless love, you gain control of your emotions. Selfless love can only be located in a heart without condemnation or blame. Happiness comes from losing yourself in the welfare of others. Selfishness leads to pride, envy, and resentment. Selflessness leads to humility, compassion, and serenity. As you eliminate selfish desires, replacing them with consideration and service to others, you'll realize lasting joy.

I can't count the number of times in the past year that I've said to myself, *no self, no problem.* Learning this concept has immensely improved my life. It's been shocking to see how frequently I thought I had a problem and the moment I removed self from the equation, the problem disappeared. I'm not saying it's an easy concept to understand, accept, or adopt, but I am saying my experience has been a happier, more fulfilled, less stressful life since implementing it.

Prejudice is an inflexible judgment. It's an unfavorable opinion formed without sufficient knowledge. It includes the attitudes of contempt and loathing. It's an unreasonable attitude of hostility aimed at an individual or group.

LOVE HAS NO PREJUDICE

To experience a world of love and peace, prejudice must be eliminated. Prejudice is a form of hate that leads to slander and violence. When prejudice is present, cruelty is not far behind. We often feel we aren't guilty of prejudice until we take a closer look at its meaning.

Most stereotypes are a form of prejudice. Indians are drunks. Jews are greedy. Blacks are lazy. Southerners are slow. Italians are mobsters. Rich people are ruthless. Mormons are polygamists. Arabs are terrorists. Those attitudes and any like them are the antithesis of love. Regardless of our differences, we're all precious human beings, each deserving the right to live our lives, within the law, as we see fit without

The attitude that "my way's right and yours is wrong" is not only ignorance but sows the seeds of conflict.

interference. Our differences can be helpful in our growth and they are something that should be celebrated rather than scorned.

Truth has no contradiction. Muslims, Hindus, Jews, Catholics, Protestants, and Buddhists each claim their religion is the right one. This leaves us with contradiction and therefore cannot be true.

Don't each of these religions teach the same principles of the importance of a blameless life, a pure heart, generosity, forgiveness, honesty, doing good deeds, and love? Don't consider yourself a person of love until you bring to an end your judgments and replace them with tolerance and humility.

Having the attitude "I'm right and you're wrong" is far from love.

This is a more subtle point than you might think at first glance. It's easy to find examples of this kind of prejudice: *how dumb is it to get a tattoo? Why would anyone dye her hair pink? Can't she see that her dress is too low-cut? It's preposterous for those Amish men to wear those silly hats and grow those long beards. Anyone who wears dreadlocks must never have seen himself in a mirror. Even someone with half a brain knows abortion is wrong. War is so stupid and those Republicans are nothing more than war-mongers. Democrats want to take what the rich have worked for and give it to people too lazy to work. Only a fool would be against the death penalty.* When we accept love, we no longer have those judgmental attitudes. I'm not saying you won't still have your opinions. They will just be your opinions and not judgments on what others should or should not do. We want others to live their lives as they see fit and expect the same from them. Love doesn't discriminate, thinks no evil, is not provoked, does not behave rudely, respects and forgives all, and slanders none. Shouldn't we focus on minding our own business and concerning ourselves with questions like: "How can I improve my life and be of service?"

Having been raised in Macon, Georgia in the 1940s, I've seen the pain caused by prejudice. I've seen drinking fountains and restrooms designated for white and black. I've seen blacks forced to sit in the back of the bus. I was appalled at such treatment as a child. It is who we are that counts and not our color, language, or customs. I can't understand how Protestants and Catholics can kill each other in Ireland while worshiping the same God who teaches: "Thou shall not kill." As a young man, I was confused by the bickering among religious groups and concluded that all the people on earth warrant equal treatment and deserve to be respected. It doesn't matter if they're red, yellow, black, or white. It makes no difference what they eat, how they dress, or what language they speak. Whether they are rich or poor, tall or short, skinny or fat, sick or healthy or anything else, they are all precious living beings who deserve to live their lives in peace. How hard is it to give others the respect we want for ourselves?

A GRANDMOTHER'S LOVE

I've been blessed with love throughout my life. It's not easy finding the right words to portray the love of my grandmother. She was a shining example of selflessness and love. She made me special meals and took me to church every Sunday. After church, she'd take me to a cafeteria and let me choose whatever I wanted from the long counters of food. She let me swim in the lake and took me to good movies. She encouraged me to pick apples and pears from our trees and let me climb the pecan trees and shake the limbs so the pecans would fall to the ground. She listened to the Lone Ranger on the radio with me every night. She taught me to ride a bike and helped with my paper route. She picked me up from school on rainy days and made sure I was warm enough on cold nights. She let me go barefoot, play in the rain, jump in mud puddles, and catch fireflies in a jar. Because of the love my grandmother gave me, I can't imagine a better childhood. As you think of the people you love most, I'll wager it's the ones who are the most selfless and thoughtful to you. Once you recognize this connection, you'll want to become that kind of person.

TRUTH

My intention in this section is to expose you to ideas and principles proven to lead you to a superior life. As children, we were taught to tell the truth. Even if your parents didn't discipline you, you soon learned there were consequences for dishonesty. You found that your lies were hard to remember and eventually came back to haunt you. You discovered that you suffered emotionally and sometimes physically from your lies. As we mature, we perceive that lies are not the only form of non-truth. We begin to see that truth is clothed in details. When you omit or shade an important point, you're being deceitful and that's a form of non-truth. To twist, slant, make up, or trick is to deceive. At last we learn to live truth by giving up selfishness. Truth and love combined can cure many of the world's evils.

When I was twelve, my dad was transferred to Miramar Naval Air Station in San Diego, California. I got a job distributing flyers to the homes in our area to earn spending money. We lived in a mountainous region with remote canyons. My pay was determined by how many flyers I distributed. They were delivered to me in giant bundles. I figured out that the easiest way to make money was throwing some of the bundles into the canyons, assuming they would never be found. The bundles were exceptionally heavy and it was difficult carrying them to my personal dumpsite. One day, I arrived home to find my dad waiting for me with the boss from the flyer company. Someone had seen me dumping and reported it. My first punishment was being required to pay back the money I'd received. Next, my dad escorted me to my dumpsite and made me retrieve the bundles. It was far more difficult dragging bundles up the canyon than it had been tossing them down. It took six hours to haul them all out. When we got back home, my dad restricted me to my room for two weeks. This was my painful introduction to the consequences of not being truthful and honest.

My dad taught me about truth and honesty on another important occasion. I was a grown man, visiting him at his home in Las Vegas. He loved golf and he and I were out playing a round together. I spotted a brand new ball in the rough. I didn't see anyone else around to claim it, so I picked it up and started to put it in my bag. My dad asked what I was doing and I told him I had found a ball and I didn't see anyone around to whom it belonged. He said, "Son, there's one thing you do know—it isn't *yours.*" That may sound a bit harsh, but it sure made a point with me and I left the ball where I had found it.

A manifestation of truth is honesty.

When you're truthful with yourself, you see things as they are and not the way you want them to be.

Living truth entails ridding oneself of all that's not genuine. We can become truthful with a conscientious effort, but our mastery of truth must originate from the heart. To live in truth requires patience and practice.

A life of truth has no delusion; it admits that your difficulties are of your own creation. To live in truth requires that we work to improve ourselves and that we not be bothered by the sins of others. Self-pity comes from ignorance. You can't avoid cause and effect nor can you escape their consequences. Your thoughts and desires lead to your deeds. People of truth can be recognized by their moral maturity. If you cling to self, truth will evade you. The highway to truth is paved with love, patience, compassion, gentleness, humility, charity, modesty, and a lack of self-indulgence.

QUIZ	HOW MUCH DOES HONESTY MATTER TO YOU?

1 You are good friends with two people who are dating. You know the guy is cheating. The girl suspects. She asks you if he is. What do you do?

> **a** Tell her yes.
>
> **b** Tell her no, so he doesn't get in trouble and she doesn't get hurt.
>
> **c** Say you don't really know for sure.

2 Your friend tells you that she is madly in love with a guy you can't stand. Do you tell her that you don't like him?

> **a** Yes, I probably couldn't hide my feelings for long anyway.
>
> **b** No, I'd act like I did.
>
> **c** I'd act cool with it but I'd point out the things I don't like.

3 One of your friends has terrible breath. You . . .

a Pull him aside and let him know he needs to step up his brush game.

b Offer him some gum or breath mints and hope he gets the hint.

c Say nothing because you don't want to hurt his feelings.

4 All your friends are going to the beach and want you to come, too, but you have to work— and it's the most beautiful weather you've seen for weeks. You . . .

a Call in sick and hang out with my friends because friendship is so important.

b Suck it up and just go to work—there'll be other great days.

5 You've got a paper due tomorrow but you party with friends instead. You know your teacher usually knocks a grade off for each day a paper is late, so you . . .

a Tell the teacher I was really sick and ask the teacher to give me an extra day without penalty.

b Say the paper isn't ready because I really want to do a great job (which I do but I don't say anything about partying)—and I ask for one more day without a penalty to my grade. It can't hurt to ask.

c Don't say anything and just turn the paper in a day late.

6 You are in the car with one of your friends when he dents another car as he's parking— and does not leave his name. Later you find out the other car belongs to another friend of yours who you also like. You . . .

a Tell my friend who was driving that he should tell the other friend what he did.

b Tell the other friend whose car was dented what happened, but tell him not to let anyone know who told him.

c Don't say anything to anybody—either way, if I speak up, I might lose a friend.

7 On quizzes like this one, you try to figure out the answers you think will get you the best score, instead of answering all the questions honestly.

a Always.
b Sometimes.
c Never.

| SCORE | Count up your points, then flip to the end of the chapter to find out what your score means. |

1 a. 3; b. 1; c. 2   **5** a 1; b. 2; c. 3

2 a 3; b. 1; c. 2   **6** a. 3; b. 2; c. 1

3 a 3; b. 2; c. 1   **7** a. 1; b. 2; c. 3

4 a. 1; b. 3

THOUGHT

It's disgraceful that we live in an advanced era and still don't teach our children the significance of their thoughts. Don't you find it strange that you've gone through school and never had a class on thoughts? Children listen to music, read books, watch television, and go to movies that shape their thinking but are unaware of the influence those activities have on their lives.

Every facet of life is determined by our thinking, yet we're not taught how to think.

Your thoughts can become actualized. If you're happy, it's because you dwell in happy thoughts and if you're sad, it's because you dwell in sad thoughts. Wise people control their thinking, but fools are controlled by their thinking. You're who you are today because of your past thinking and your current thinking will shape your future. Successes happen in the mind before they become reality.

I see clearly how my thinking affected my life and I'm sure the same will be true for you. In school, when I thought I wasn't good at something, I allowed it to become a self-fulfilling prophecy. Now I recognize I could have been good at whatever I wanted had I changed my thinking.

YOU BECOME WHAT YOU THINK ABOUT

If you think you can, you can. If you think you can't, you can't. It's all in your state of mind. Good thoughts bring good results. Bad thoughts bring bad results.

Never say or think anything about yourself that you don't want to be true.

In baseball, when I thought I would strike out, I usually did. In golf, when I thought I would make a birdie, I usually did. If I asked a girl out and thought she would accept, she usually did. If you want someone to like you, think that they will.

This one act alone will vastly improve your life. Most people don't comprehend that their thoughts are their truth. By improving your thinking, you can place yourself on the road to success and happiness. All that you aspire to begins with your thoughts.

Only think thoughts that you want to be true.

You're precisely where you are today because of your thoughts, actions, and choices. This isn't to say that bad things don't sometimes happen to good people. Rare diseases happen and accidents happen that are out of your control. Those are the exceptions and not the rule. Even in those cases, it's not the circumstance that determines the outcome but your thoughts and actions in those circumstances. We

Until you accept responsibility for your situation, you can't improve it.

know that your hopes and wishes will not decide your future, but most assuredly your thoughts will. If you're discontent, the satisfaction you desire must come from within you. Look to yourself for the cause of your happiness or sorrow. If you suffer, it's because you haven't corrected your thinking. To whine or complain is not to understand.

As long as you imagine you're a victim, you condemn yourself to misery.

Your external world will improve in direct proportion to your improved thinking. Rake the garden of your mind and purge it of all unhealthy and selfish thoughts, replacing them with thoughts of forgiveness, generosity, and service. The joy you crave can't come from outside of you.

Any time you're faced with a harmful emotion such as anger, jealousy, or hate, you can eliminate it by simply altering your thinking. Eliminate evil and hurtful thoughts, replacing them with ones that are healthy. Constantly think about the qualities you long to possess and over time they will become yours. Constantly affirm that you are already the person that you want to be. Peace and happiness are certain to follow.

Every time you substitute a good thought for a bad one, you improve your world.

ATTACHMENT

Our lives are full of paradoxes and attachment falls into that category. Frequently, we find we must do the opposite of what seems logical to achieve a goal. For example, in golf, if you want the ball to go up, you have to hit down. When driving on an icy road, if you start to skid, you must turn in the direction you're sliding to regain control. To prevail in a disagreement, you must encourage the other person to say all he or she has to say before trying to make your point, temporally giving up your attachment to your point of view and actively listening. To make a good first impression, you have to show the other person you're impressed with him or her.

You achieve by giving up and lose by holding on. This isn't saying you don't have a desired result; it's simply that you're not attached to it.

I've played golf for thirty years being attached to my score. Because of that attachment, I've cursed, thrown clubs, quit, pouted, complained, and argued on the golf course. After moving to Hawaii, I met Kenny Springer, a golf professional who became my teacher and friend. He taught me to play to have fun regardless of my score. I began noticing that the more I was attached to my score, the worse I played. I frequently didn't enjoy the game and was unpleasant to be around during and after a bad round. Little by little, I developed a happy attitude regardless of score. Eventually, I was able to detach fully and was no longer troubled about my score. My game immediately improved. My goal had been breaking 80 and I did it about half the time. Since then, most of my rounds have been less than 80 with some in the low 70s. I've had more fun, practiced less, been told I'm more enjoyable to play with, and played the best golf of my life. It's amazing how everything improved once I detached from my score.

The more you're attached to a result, the less chance you have of accomplishing it.

Our attachments often consist of possessions such as cars, boats, and houses, as well as non-material items such as jobs, titles, and people. None of those are permanent and who we are is not our possessions, jobs, or friends. Attachments are a form of insecurity. By relinquishing what's not permanent, we find joy and peace. The more secure we become in who we are, the less we need attachments.

SORROW/DIFFICULTIES/TEMPTATIONS

As your belief in the preeminence of good strengthens, you'll begin looking at sorrows and difficulties as teachers, helping you navigate your way to a better life. Every obstacle, even the minor ones, can be an opportunity to improve your inner life because every difficulty reveals an inward flaw.

Each difficulty you encounter is an occasion to grow spiritually.

We must learn to accept our pain or inconvenience and grow from it without blaming or complaining. For example, if you wake up with a hangover, use it as the reason to stop drinking to excess. If you're trying to fix one of your electronic gadgets and it's not going well, look at it as an opportunity to learn patience. If you injure yourself doing a home improvement project, see it as a chance to learn to work with more care and caution. Our suffering is minimized when we view it as a form of discipline and it's eliminated as we achieve selflessness.

Let's look at the example of a married man being tempted by a seductive woman. He can't be tempted unless he's open to her and gives in to the thought of being with her.

Thoughts only have the power you give them.

When he gives in to temptation, he immediately begins to suffer because of his longing to spend time with her. Once he's satisfied his desire, his anguish continues as he seeks to repeat those pleasures. Even when he stops his imprudent behavior, his suffering continues because of guilt and remorse. The same pattern follows all forms of excess and self-indulgence. Where there's selfishness, lust, and deception, there's misery, torment, and pain. We can't acquire the goodness of life until we're no longer dominated by our animal instincts.

It's wisest to resist the first desire rather than try and satisfy all those that follow.

CONTENTMENT

It's clear that contentment is rare when you observe that most people are dissatisfied with who they are, where they are, and with what they have. The problem with this state of mind is they're not enjoying the present, which is all that's real. Setting goals to advance your future position makes sense but not at the cost of anguish in the present.

Being content is accepting your current situation for what it is, including friendships, possessions, and career. It's not passivity and is in fact quite proactive. Accepting what is requires the discipline of mind to recognize that the present is your reality and the courage to embrace it while making plans to improve your future. By adopting this posture, you'll be able to enjoy the present. The contented soul allows the spirit to renew itself. Contented people live longer and enjoy better health than those who live a frantic life. Success and peace find their way to the contented soul. Living in a calm state is the hallmark of contentment. Discontent is resistance to the present and that's foolhardy.

To be content is to experience joy and satisfaction.

Contentment is achievable once you establish how much is enough and what you care about most. How much money is enough to live the way you want to live and allow you to retire when you're ready? How many children, houses, and cars are enough? How many hours of work and recreation are enough? If you want to maintain your weight, you need to know how many calories are enough. Knowing how much is enough in all areas leads to contentment. Once you decide what you care about most, you can put your efforts toward that end and happiness is sure to follow. You'll know what you truly care about by your actions. The man who says he cares most about his family yet spends fifteen-hour days and weekends working is not being honest. Determine what you care about and then make sure your actions reflect those decisions.

QUIZ **ARE YOU COOL WITH WHO YOU ARE?**

1 At least once a week I try to find something to do just for me—because I like doing it and I know it will make me feel better.

- **a** Never or hardly at all
- **b** Sometimes
- **c** Frequently
- **d** Very often

2 When I feel really sad, I'd rather be alone than with other people, even my friends, because I don't want to be a pain.

- **a** Never or hardly at all
- **b** Sometimes

c Frequently
d Very often

3 I feel comfortable telling my friends what I want, and when I need help from them. I don't hide my feelings.

a Never or hardly at all
b Sometimes
c Frequently
d Very often

4 Every time I look in the mirror I notice something about me that I wish I could change.

a Never or hardly at all
b Sometimes
c Frequently
d Very often

5 I try to give other people compliments—sometimes I even look past their bad parts to find something good to say.

a Never or hardly at all
b Sometimes
c Frequently
d Very often

6 If I decide to lose some weight and then eat a bunch of cookies—or decide to start exercising

QUIZ	**ARE YOU COOL WITH WHO YOU ARE?** *(continued)*

but then skip a few days—I feel so bad I give up on the whole thing.

- **a** Never or hardly at all
- **b** Sometimes
- **c** Frequently
- **d** Very often

7 If I make a mistake, I apologize and I find myself saying "I'm sorry" a lot—sometimes even when I don't think it's really my fault.

- **a** Never or hardly at all
- **b** Sometimes
- **c** Frequently
- **d** Very often

SCORE	Count up your points, then flip to the end of the chapter to find out what your score means.

1 a 1; b 2; c 3; d 4   **5** a 1; b 2; c 3; d 4

2 a 4; b 3; c 2; d 1   **6** a 4; b 3; c 2; d 1

3 a 1; b 2; c 3; d 4   **7** a 4; b 3; c 2; d 1

4 a 4; b 3; c 2; d 1

THE VOICE

Controlling your speech is the beginning of wisdom. I'm sure you recall times when you said something hastily that caused you heartache and pain. By gaining control of our speech, we can experience a higher level of peace and happiness. To attain mastery of the tongue is an enormous task but attainable and worth the effort. *Don't say anything about someone that you wouldn't say to his or her face.* Hasty words, bitter retorts, slander, gossip, and unkind speech all lead to misery, pain, hurt, and damaged relationships.

Support friends if they're absent. If an idle mind is the Devil's workshop, idle chatter is one of his tools. The wise course of action is to talk with a generous purpose or remain silent. How many times have you gotten in trouble for something you didn't say? Silence is a cure for many ills. Say only those things that benefit yourself or others.

FORGIVENESS

The practice of forgiveness is a station on the road to enlightenment. Many years ago, I was president of Pasatiempo Golf Club and one of my responsibilities was running board meetings and annual elections. During one of the elections, a past board member said some harsh things about me in front of the members. I was humiliated even though I was easily re-elected. From that night forward, I resented this person and held a grudge against him. I refused to look at or speak to him.

I experienced stress every time I saw this person or heard his name. I occasionally altered my plans to avoid him. The more upset I became, the more it seemed to please him. After five years of this, I decided to forgive him. The next time I saw him, I smiled and asked how he was doing. You could have knocked him over with a feather. From that point forward, I held no grudge and only wished the best for him. I felt better about myself and had no more anxiety in his presence. In retrospect, I should have forgiven him immediately because I'd have saved myself five years of grief. You know you're learning to forgive when you can deal with old grudges without anxiety. If everyone practiced forgiveness, it would change the world. Forgiveness is a gift you give yourself.

I want you to learn from this story that resentment and grudges harm the person holding them.

WRAPPING UP LOVE AND TRUTH

By being brave enough to pursue love and truth, you'll one day break free of doubt, worry, and fear. You won't second-guess yourself. Your struggles will be rewarded with contentment. Through this process, you'll defeat your inward foes, leaving pain and anguish behind. The majority don't understand the prize you now have within your reach, but those that do live uncommonly happy lives. You can master the lessons of life just as you succeeded with your education in school. It's time to lift your mind above purely worldly desires. As you ascend to this new level, you'll leave evil behind. Your belief in justice and fairness will become your shield, allowing you to withstand the arrows of hate and spears of prejudice. You'll know that your condition is the result of your own thoughts and actions. You may experience turmoil or despair but you now know they are only a prelude to the wonderful things to come. You will be able to experience them without complaining, knowing each trial you overcome is leading you to higher ground. Continue to study and apply all aspects of truth and love and one day you will awake to find you have become it.

CONCLUSION

Mentors

You're entering one of the most significant periods of your life, where the decisions you'll soon be making will have long-term consequences. You'll decide on a career, who to marry, where to live, and when and if you'll have children. Given that you don't have experience in these vital matters, it's important that you seek the wise counsel of those who do. My mentors trained me on how to succeed and yours can do the same for you. Seek advice from the people you admire and respect before making important decisions. Finding a mentor can be a daunting task. One of the reasons this book was written was to provide aid for young people without a mentor. I suggest you take an inventory of the successful people in your circle of family and friends as a first act to find a suitable mentor. A thriving grandparent can often be the perfect mentor. You may require different mentors for different needs. One may be knowledgeable about real estate and another may be able to consult with you about dating and marriage. You need to be courageous enough to approach successful people you meet. You'll need to use the human relations skills you learned in chapter 1 to woo the mentor of your choice.

Nothing will cause you to lose a mentor's help faster than not following the advice he or she gives you. If you're considering marriage, seek the advice of someone you respect who's been happily married. If you're thinking of buying a house, find someone who has successfully bought and sold houses. In every case, be sure it's someone with nothing to gain by the advice he or she gives you; for example, if you're going to buy a house, your realtor would have a lot to gain. Find someone who has no stake in the game and someone who has your best interest at heart. I was fortunate to find a mentor who had been successful in almost every aspect of his life. None of the questions I asked seemed beyond his experience and his recommendations were always valuable. Now that I'm a mentor I understand why mine told me that they were willing to help me because I immediately did exactly what they suggested. Mentors won't continue to help you if you only do some of what they suggest. Follow their suggestions to the letter and they'll keep on helping you.

The essential ingredient to getting and keeping a mentor is to do exactly what the mentor suggests and in a timely fashion. Give your mentor full credit for the successes you have.

Getting In Is Easier Than Getting Out

In my twenties, I didn't understand how easy it was to get into things compared to how difficult it could be to get out. This information will help you because you can apply it to some of the important decisions you'll soon face. I want you to understand this truth so you'll use care before making important decisions. Marriage is a good case in point because getting married is easy, but some of life's most complicated and distressing moments accompany a divorce. Buying is easy while selling is usually more difficult. Borrowing money is easy; paying it back can be easier said than done. Receiving a credit card is easy; paying the charges in full monthly is often a problem. Most of life's vices seem enjoyable and are easy to indulge in, but all of them become progressively more difficult to quit. Be cautious before getting into something by considering what's required to get out.

Reputation and Public Identity

My mentor said, "All we have is our reputation." It's vital to maintain a favorable reputation. Your reputation and public identity are formed by the way you help people and the way you function in a group. One way to be held in high esteem is doing more for people than they anticipate. One of your friends may ask you to watch her children for her while she goes to a doctor's appointment. While watching the children, you also help her by doing the dishes, making a meal, or tidying up the children's room. A second way is accomplishing things faster than expected. When your computer guru tells you it will take five or six hours to complete a job and does the job in half the time, you are favorably impressed. Honesty, integrity, and being a person whose word is his or her bond all build a favorable public identity. You will enhance your reputation by the things you do for

> **Be the person who deals in facts and doesn't make assumptions.**

others that open opportunities for them. An example would be arranging an interview for someone with a company where he or she wishes to be employed or helping someone find the right financial advisor. It would also include referring someone to people who could improve the quality of his or her life, such as a good doctor, dentist, or other key service provider.

A Few More Insights

Assumptions get people into trouble. Let's say you're leaving for a three-week trip and you assume your roommate locked the house, only to find when you return that he or she didn't, and you have been burglarized. You notice a small lump in your breast, but assume it's nothing to worry about, then you require major surgery a year later. You have friends visit with their small children and you assume the gate to the pool is closed, but it wasn't and you find one of the children almost drowns. You assume you're sober enough to drive only to find yourself in a cell for the night with a DUI. When you assume, you usually make an ASS out of U and ME. Don't assume. Learn to deal only in facts.

Don't take things personally.

You'll discover that most of the annoying things people do have little or nothing to do with you and are merely the way they behave regardless of with whom they're dealing. If someone does not return your call, it is about him or her and not you. If people don't respond to an invitation to your party, it's about them and not you. You will have a much happier life if you don't worry about what other people do. It's rarely personal.

Make it your practice to "pass it on down."

Sharing is a survival skill. Don't let the good things you experience end with you. Share them with those you love and want to help. My mentor had a pair of cufflinks he received from his father before they left Turkey in the late 1800s. One day, he gave them to me, telling me the story behind them, how much they had meant to him, and how much I meant to him. I was touched deeply by this gesture. That was twenty-five years

When you find life difficult and stressful, think of it as a "bumpy road."

ago, and now I find myself giving some of my prized belongings to those I love so they can enjoy the feelings such an act gave me. Share good ideas with those you care about and give meaningful things to those you love or want to help.

What do you do when the road gets too bumpy? Slow down until you get back on smooth pavement. For example, let's say your finances are stretched, your car needs repair, and your health is beginning to suffer. Each of these is a whispering and the message is that you need to

Take solace in the fact that right efforts will eventually produce right results.

slow down, step back, rethink, and regroup. Take each situation that is out of balance and figure out how to put it back where it should be. Get off the gas and on the brake until you can get back to smooth pavement. When you're at your wit's end, it's time to slow down.

Put away your criticisms, complaints, anger, blame, doubts, and fear and remember that nothing happens to you that is not for your growth or benefit. Your difficulties can be conquered if they're correctly dealt with,

Keep in mind that your journey is just beginning.

so there's no cause for alarm. Your unhappiness comes from a mistaken state of mind. The superior life you yearn for will be brought about by expanding your thoughts, words, and deeds. You can have the joy, peace, and happiness you long for when you personify selflessness, humility, compassion, kindness, love, sympathy, and patience.

1. You've read about life's most important lessons, but they will do you no good unless you apply them. This is where you decide if you're willing to pursue success and happiness or if you will settle for a mediocre life. You've been given all the tools to realize your dreams. There's no magic wand and no one else can do it for you.

2. Remember that the first step to any accomplishment is desire and the greater the desire, the greater the commitment. How badly do you want your aspirations to be fulfilled?

3. Are you the person who'll put this book down after a single reading or are you that rare person who knows success and happiness come with

a price and that price is effort and intelligent action?

④ If you want a rich, fulfilling life, go back to chapter 1 and start adopting each suggestion about human relations; keep at it until you have incorporated each of them into your life. Then move on to habits and do the same for each succeeding chapter until you have addressed each discipline in the book. If you're willing to follow that plan, your success is assured and your life will be meaningful and memorable.

Whisperings

A whispering is a subtle communication that has significance. People who pay attention to whisperings escape a lot of grief. Those who recognize whisperings know that the first sign of a hurricane is a change in the wind and that gathering gray clouds may be the prelude to a flood. Some people must be hit over the head before they wake up while others avoid suffering by acting on whisperings. The following maxims have been tested and found to be true. I have benefited from these whisperings for many years and trust you will profit from them as well. Each requires some thought to avoid missing the deeper meaning. Take your time reading them and refer to them often. As your thinking evolves, the meaning of the whisperings will take on greater importance in your life.

1. Never think or say anything about yourself that you don't want to be true.
2. The small precedes the great.
3. People who feel sorry for themselves, should.
4. There's no right way to do a wrong thing.
5. Non-accomplishment resides in continuous postponement.
6. The fruit of self-indulgence is unhappiness.
7. Dread drains while faith inspires.
8. If you want to co-exist with people, celebrate their world.
9. It's not what you have but who you have in your life that matters.
10. Be careful when you're around people who don't attract friendships.
11. All that I give is given to myself.
12. A diamond is a piece of coal that stuck to the job.
13. Age is a high price to pay for maturity.
14. Pleasure comes from outside of you; joy comes from within.
15. All evil is ignorant.

16. The weak become strong by attaching value to small things and doing them correctly.

17. There is no place to hide a sin where your conscience can't see it.

18. Cheerfulness and unselfishness are close friends.

19. A closed mouth gathers no feet.

20. Making a living is not the same as making a life.

21. It's a lot easier getting in than getting out.

22. An old young person will be a young old person.

23. Failure is a prerequisite to success.

24. Who gossips to you will gossip of you.

25. The faintest ink is stronger than the clearest memory.

26. A wish is a desire with no effort to realize it.

27. Nothing causes as much pain as too much pleasure.

28. Enjoy the good things of life when available and make them last as long as you can.

29. Knowing is better than wondering.

30. You can't be outstanding if you're one of the many.

31. Anything that's wrong gets worse the longer you delay correcting it.

32. To know and not to do is still not to know.

33. It's easier to resist the first vice than to try to satisfy all that follow.

34 Remember how important other people's futures are to them.

35 Drawing lines doesn't keep others out; they keep you in.

36 People who talk just of themselves think only of themselves.

37 The things that hurt may instruct.

38 A man convinced against his will is of the same opinion still.

39 As long as you look to others for fulfillment, you'll never be fulfilled.

40 The more you do of what you've done, the more you'll have of what you've got.

41 We don't see things as they are but as we are.

42 Wise men don't belabor their point and people who belabor their point aren't wise.

43 Worry is soul suicide.

44 When you realize you're on the wrong road, don't go to the end before you turn around.

45 Don't expect trouble as trouble tends not to disappoint.

46 There's no feeling more degrading than self-pity.

47 Wisdom is found in self-mastery.

48 Good luck is preparedness and opportunity coming together.

49 Joy comes from a task well done.

50 You can spend your life drawing lines or crossing them.

51 He who knows all knows nothing; he who assumes all is foolish.

52 Care about people's approval and you'll be their prisoner.

53 Believe in yourself and you won't have to try to convince others.

54 If you realize you have enough, you are truly rich.

55 What you don't know can hurt you.

56 To have peace, you must harness the wild steed of desire.

57 Those who are feared are hated.

58 Grief often treads on the heels of pleasure.

59 He that cannot obey cannot command.

60 Don't do anything you would not have known.

61 Virtue and Happiness are Mother and Daughter.

62 The time to repair the roof is when the sun is out.

63 In the middle of difficulty lies opportunity.

64 Wealth that is shared creates more wealth.

65 Good judgment comes from experience and much experience comes from bad judgment.

66 Great love and achievements involve great risk.

67 Being kind is more important than being right.

68 Ignorance is not bliss.

THE BEST BOOKS I'VE EVER READ

The Greatest Salesman in the World by Og Mandino

How to Have Confidence and Power in Dealing with People by Les Giblin

Think and Grow Rich by Napoleon Hill

The Wisdom of James Allen, Volumes 1, 2, and 3 by James Allen

The Power of Now by Eckhart Tolle

The Four Agreements by Miguel Ruiz

Men Are from Mars, Women Are from Venus by John Gray

The Power of Positive Thinking by Norman Vincent Peale

How to Win Friends and Influence People by Dale Carnegie

● HOW THOUGHTFUL ARE YOU?

What your score means:

If you scored between 12 and 15 points, you almost always think of others and are a pretty selfless person with healthy self-esteem. You realize that showing kindness and love to those who surround you will make you feel happy and good about yourself.

If you scored between 9 and 11 points, you consider other people, but you hold back at times. You're on the right path to truly being selfless, but you may need a little help. You still worry about what other people think, but not too much. Look to your mentors and people you admire to help you become more thoughtful and loving.

If you scored between 5 and 8 points, you have a hard time being selfless and thoughtful. It's hard not to be selfish sometimes, but it will benefit you in the long run to think of someone besides yourself. Try to stop worrying about what other people think of you; be comfortable with yourself. Next time you have the option to do something nice for someone else—do it! You'll probably like how you feel afterward.

● HOW MUCH DOES HONESTY MATTER TO YOU?

What your score means:

If you scored between 14 and 21 points, your instincts are good—you're pretty honest. Even though it isn't always easy to speak the truth, people will like you for it and trust you as a friend.

If you scored between 7 and 13 points, you tend to avoid confrontations and take the easy path. You might want to work on leveling with others and yourself. If you start noticing it's hard for others to trust you, there may be a good reason. You may think you're getting away with stuff, but it could come back to haunt you later.

● **ARE YOU COOL WITH WHO YOU ARE?**

What your score means:

If you scored more than 17 points, you think you're pretty cool—and you should! You are—and people who like themselves a lot tend to have more friends and do better in life. If you don't like yourself, how can you expect others to? So keep on patting yourself on the back—it only gets better.

If you scored below 17 points, you are cooler than you think—so don't be so hard on yourself. It helps to focus on what you are doing right more than what you are doing wrong. You'll discover that when you start noticing all the good things you are doing, so will other people.

J. R. Parrish went from being a milkman to a multimillionaire. In 1974, he founded J. R. Parrish Inc., a commercial real estate company in Silicon Valley. He ran the company based on the premise that to succeed in life, you must treat people with fairness and respect, a premise that not only won him friends, but made him a fortune. J. R. spent the next twenty-five years studying and teaching his employees and brokers about human relations. The company grew to be a huge success and one of the premier real estate brokerage firms in Silicon Valley. J. R. retired in 1999.

Today, he and his wife Lisa live in one of the most idyllic spots in the Hawaiian Islands, on their own coffee plantation. He continues to support the ideals he believes in through his foundation.